PRAISE FOR
THE PREDICTIVE HIRING MODEL
Six Disciplines to Get It Right Every Time

Hiring the right people is one of the toughest and most important decisions a leader can make. The Predictive Hiring Model replaces the guesswork with a proven, data-driven system designed to help you attract and retain top talent. Chad Carter doesn't just talk theory—he gives you practical tools you can start using today. If you're serious about building a winning team, this book will be your hiring playbook.

—**Michael Hyatt**, New York Times Bestselling Author and Business Coach

Wow! This is an outstanding book! I truly don't say that lightly. I believe it is one of the best books I have read on the subject of hiring and I will be recommending it to my clients. The Predictive Hiring Model resonates with my own principles from years of selecting talent at Chick-fil-A.

In The Predictive Hiring Model, *Chad Carter has written the guidebook on how to hire talent. If you follow his systematic, repeatable process, you will transform your organization and enjoy the results all along the way. Follow Chad's step-by-step guidance to help you and your team hire the talent that will help your organization win.*

—**Dee Ann Turner**, 3x Best-Selling Author, VP, Talent, Chick-fil-A, Inc. (retired)

This is a game-changer! I've been blessed over my 25+ year career as a retained executive recruiter to be focused on the vital competency of hiring A+ talent. With that in mind, I can say with conviction that The Predictive Hiring Model *is exactly what leaders need today. The wisdom that Chad Carter has captured in this powerful book equips decision-makers with practical, proven strategies to attract, hire, and build exceptionally high-performing leaders and teams. Chad's expertise, approach, and heart for doing this wisely make this an indispensable resource for anyone serious about hiring right the first time.*

—**Steve Hayes**, CHRO and Retained Executive Recruiter (retired)

I've been waiting for this exact book for 20 years! I've urged Chad Carter to share his unparalleled expertise in a book, and now, The Predictive Hiring Model *is finally here. It's hands down the best hiring book I've ever read—practical, insightful, and actionable. This book is a must-read for every hiring manager in your organization. Chad Carter has masterfully taken what many of us struggle with and made it accessible to leaders at every level. If you want to consistently hire the best, this book will be your new go-to guide.*

—**Michael Moore**, Managing Partner, Treeline Bamboo Partners

Clearly written, evidence-based, and packed with practical guidance from real-life experience, The Predictive Hiring Model *is a must-read for anyone serious about building top-performing teams. I witnessed firsthand Chad›s relentless pursuit of excellence and his ability to challenge the status quo. It was during this time that* The Predictive Hiring Model *was born—a transformational, systematic process that became our foundation for selecting top talent. By hiring the best, we cultivated a winning culture that gave us a clear competitive advantage.*

In today's fast-paced world, where organizations are constantly searching for an edge, this book offers the roadmap to creating your preferred future. The Predictive Hiring Model *equips you with the tools to make smarter decisions and position your organization for long-term success.*

—**Debra J. Shecterle**, CHRO, Doane Pet Care & Y-12 National Security Complex (retired)

It's no secret that hiring and retaining the right people has become problematic in today's work culture. Chad Carter's The Predictive Hiring Model *provides six clear guidelines in a concise and well-written book to help you and your organization identify, hire, and retain the right people - every time. I highly recommend every business leader read this!*
—**Matt Litton**, Author & Bestselling Collaborative Writer

Chad Carter is a true expert in the art and science of hiring transformational talent. In The Predictive Hiring Model, *he distills decades of experience into a clear, repeatable process that helps organizations make better hiring decisions with confidence. His insights into predictive hiring are not theory—they are practical, actionable strategies that lead to long-term success. If you're serious about building high-performing teams, this book is a must-read.*
—**Al Lopus**, Cofounder & Board Chair, Best Christian Workplaces

Chad Carter's book, The Predictive Hiring Model, *provides a masterclass for anyone who has to make a hiring decision. Outlining the six disciplines essential to hiring, he teaches you how to select the best person every time. You will also learn to avoid the pitfalls that can quickly derail your long-term goals. Now is the time to understand and embrace the disciplines that consistently lead to successful selections and transformational outcomes. This is a critical book for everyone in a leadership role!*
—**Tami Heim**, President and CEO, Christian Leadership Alliance

I've been an eyewitness to Chad Carter's focus, which always put people first. As an undergraduate student at Lee University, I knew of Chad's love for people; therefore, I placed him in a human resources internship with a clothing manufacturer. Chad shared with me a story where a line seamstress called him to her machine and inquired about his internship. She said the only intern she knew of was a medical intern, so what kind of intern was he. With a tremendous amount of respect for her, he replied, "I'm a business intern, and I'm here to learn from you." He knows that people are the foundation for exceptional results.

For better than 20 years in college administration, I always told my team that hiring was our most important function. If you care deeply about people, your career, your company, and your culture, you must develop the vital competency of hiring right. The Predictive Hiring Model is infused with hard-fought, practical wisdom that every business owner, CEO, and hiring manager needs. Ask yourself, "What if I had a hiring process that predicted high-performing talent every time?" Chad's experience, research, and breadth of knowledge are blended together in this textbook which helps you hire right the first time. The Predictive Hiring Model provides a remarkable process that blends proven strategy, practical insights, and a people-first approach to hiring right.

—**Dr. Dewayne Thompson**, Dean, School of Business, Lee University (retired)

As owners of an executive recruiting firm, we know firsthand how critical hiring the right people is to the success of any organization, and we've seen how transformative Chad Carter's Predictive Hiring Model Workshop can be. He has now taken his wealth of knowledge, practical tools, proven assessments, and real-world common sense and packaged it all into a must-read book that we view as an essential guide for leaders, business owners, and hiring managers who are serious about building high-performing teams.

This book doesn't just teach you how to hire better—it equips you with a step-by-step framework to consistently predict success in your hires, reduce costly missteps, and create a culture of excellence. Whether you're new to hiring or a seasoned professional, Chad's insights will elevate your hiring process and, ultimately, your business results. The Predictive Hiring Model is an indispensable resource for anyone who wants to win at hiring.

—**Neal Joseph**, Founding Partner & Senior Advisor, and **Dr. Rich Kidd**, Managing Partner, Mission:Leadership LLC

Like Chad Carter, I've spent my career breaking down complex challenges into structured, repeatable processes that drive success. The Predictive Hiring Model is more than just a book—it is a complete blueprint for building high-performing teams with a systematic hiring approach. Chad's insights reflect wisdom gained from decades of hands-on experience, offering a practical roadmap to hiring with confidence and consistency. If you want your organization to repeatedly select the right talent and build a winning team, The Predictive Hiring Model is an indispensable resource.
—**Harold Roe**, Founder and CEO, Employee Prosperity Partners, and #1 Bestselling Author, *Maximum Prosperity*

Finally, Chad Carter has put it into a book! After decades of hiring experience, we now have the benefit of Chad's distilled wisdom and knowledge that will take the guesswork and gamble out of your hiring opportunities. I have personally and professionally benefited from using this model where we accelerated the predictability of each new hire. If you're happy and satisfied with making mistakes, wasting time, and eroding morale, then this book is not for you. Alternatively, if you're disciplined, willing to trust and follow the process, and want to step away from the 'hit or miss' outcomes of your current hiring practices, I highly recommend The Predictive Hiring Model.
—**Craig Warner**, Executive Director, The Gideons International (former)

Ultimately, every business is a people business, which means you will go as far as you can get with the people you hire, train, manage, motivate, and retain. In his latest book, The Predictive Hiring Model, Chad Carter shares decades of experience, expertise, and insights to this foundational element of leadership as you consider how to grow your business in healthy and sustainable ways.
—**Scott Prickett**, Executive Advisor & Author

THE PREDICTIVE HIRING MODEL

Six Disciplines to Get It Right Every Time

CHAD CARTER

WCG PUBLISHING

THE PREDICTIVE HIRING MODEL:
Six Disciplines to Get It Right Every Time

© MMXXV by Chad Carter. All rights reserved.

ISBN 979-8-9926211-0-5 (paperback)
ISBN 979-8-9926211-1-2 (hardback)
ISBN 979-8-9926211-2-9 (ebook)

Published by
WCG Publishing
PO Box 22184, Chattanooga, TN 37422
WatermanCG.com | 423-208-1792

Printed in the United States of America

Book design by Fishergate, Inc.

All rights reserved. No portion of this publication may be reproduced, stored in a retrieval system, or transmitted in any form or by any means—electronic, mechanical, photocopy, recording, scanning, or other—except for brief quotations in critical reviews or articles, without the prior written permission of the publisher.

Bulk orders for your team? Email chadcartertn@gmail.com

CONTENTS

FOREWORD v

INTRODUCTION ix

Chapter 1 — THE PROBLEM: Why We Can't Stay Here? . . 1

Chapter 2 — THE SOLUTION:
The Six Disciplines of Predictive Hiring . . . 13

Chapter 3 — ALIGNMENT: Make the Crooked
Path Straight. 27

Chapter 4 — RECRUITMENT: Attracting the Right People. . 39

Chapter 5 — ASSESSMENT: More than a Gut Feeling. . . 59

Chapter 6 — SCREENING: Beyond the Resume 79

Chapter 7 — OFFERING: How to Seal the Deal 101

Chapter 8 — MEASURED OUTCOMES:
Quantifying Success in Our Selection 117

Chapter 9 — THE CHALLENGE:
What Action Will You Take? 123

ENDNOTES 125

ACKNOWLEDGMENTS. 127

"The Predictive Hiring Model is a systematic, repeatable process that enables hiring managers to make informed decisions and improve the quality of hires."

FOREWORD

Every business is in the people business because business is about people serving people with mutual benefit. When we get the people part wrong, we generally don't do great at business.

I've made a lot of mistakes in hiring and managing people. When I was 20 years old, I was managing over 50 people in a call center. I learned a lot by trial and error. I was working full-time while going to college and remember sitting in a Principles of Human Resource Management class enthusiastically raising my hand before finally being called upon by the professor. "Professor, I tried applying the principles from chapter 7 last week when terminating an employee for theft, but our corporate HR folks said I did it wrong. Can you help?" The professor looked bewildered and replied, "You're actually applying the . . . things from the textbook? I don't think it was meant for that. This is theory—I'd be careful rushing out and doing just like it says. You're going to have to go figure it out—and find a professional to help you." Thanks.

The real world needs systems and processes that work—theories don't cut it!

The statistics on success in recruiting, hiring, placement, and post-hire outcomes are pretty discouraging. If you're hanging out in the "bell curve" of business performance, it can feel like a roll of the dice—but with the high stakes literally being your business, budget, culture, time, emotions, and human souls! The Predictive Hiring Model can liberate you from the bell curve of mediocrity and allow you to pursue high performance and robust good health in business.

Steve Hayes, a CEO on my board of directors, repeatedly says, "I reserve the right to get smarter." That is good news! We can learn new tricks and get better. It is not random, potluck, or hopeless.

I was meeting with Chad Carter to talk about these concepts. He made a passing remark about how so many leaders fumble the ball at easy points in the process that can change the game. "Take the offer letter process, Mike. Some leaders just use dumb templates for each person, reducing a critical hire to a template! They don't call and ask the candidate 'what would matter to you if we approached you with an offer, what is most important to you in that?'" I stared at him knowing I was one of those "dumb leaders" proudly using templates.

I happened to be hiring a key person that month and tried his advice. Just before offering a job, I called the candidate and asked her what would matter most. She replied, "I'd want to know what about my background you believe most fits your needs and why you think this is a job where I will succeed. The story matters more than the rest to me." I wrote a new intro to my offer letter doing just that. She called back after receiving it, "I was in tears at how you truly see me and my talent for this organization. It meant so much to me. This is a pay cut for me, but I'm in!" Well … Chad was right. Steve was, too—there are smarter ways to hire!

The wisest CEO who ever lived said, "The one who hires a fool or who hires those passing by is like an archer who wounds everyone." (Solomon in Proverbs 26:10) When we do this stuff wrong, people suffer and often in avoidable ways. When we get it right, everyone wins.

Be encouraged. This system is going to present the opportunity to "get smarter" and change the results in your business. We use this in our business in every hiring process.

I personally believe we are called to business as a ministry and God cares about what our business does, how it does it, the impact it has on people, and our heart in the process.

Upgrade your hiring process and you'll be upgrading your business!

Press in and press on!

—MIKE SHARROW
CEO, C12 Business Forums

INTRODUCTION

What would your organization look like if you could use predictions to attract and hire the right person almost every time?

Thanks to new research, we know a lot more about making predictions than we used to, including the fact that some people are better at it than others. According to the *Harvard Business Review*, "Making accurate predictions is a learned skill, at least in part—it's something that we can all become better at with practice."[1]

That's really good news for businesses and non-profits.

More than a century before Neil Armstrong took his "one giant step for mankind," Jules Verne, a science fiction author, wrote about two men bound for the moon aboard a projectile fired from a cannon in his novel, *From Earth to the Moon*.

Wouldn't you like to predict which candidate will actually succeed in your job opportunity?

Whether it's sports, entertainment, military, for-profit businesses, or non-profit organizations, talent is the ultimate differentiator. The ability to predict and select the right talent is not just an advantage—it's a necessity.

Welcome to a transformative journey where we'll pull the curtain back and share the art and science of "The Predictive Hiring Model." You'll discover how foresight, data, and intuition come together to build exceptional teams. This book will be a field guide to unlock the future of talent selection so that every new hire proves to be a strategic step toward unparalleled organizational results.

In my sister book, *The Essentials of Hiring: The Five Attributes*, I explain "What" you need to study when considering candidates using a no-compromise approach. In this book, I explain "How" to go about discovering if the candidate is the best fit for your organization by providing you with a systematic, repeatable process called "The Predictive Hiring Model."

I have but one purpose in writing this book—to create effective organizations while helping people achieve results that glorify God.

To borrow from Bob Buford and Peter Drucker, the father of modern-day management, my greatest hope for this work is that "The fruit of [my] work grows on other people's trees."[2] As well, I hope understanding these principles releases the energy of your vision. As I've learned over decades, sharing mistakes and wrong turns provides insights that equip others to avoid repeating these experiences.

I'm personally grateful for some of my greatest influences and mentors. Some of these I've met and enjoyed their company and others whose writing significantly influenced my own. In some cases, I've studied them so closely that I don't know where their thoughts end and mine begin. Some of these are Peter Drucker, Jim Collins, Dr. Dewayne Thompson, Dr. Paul Conn, Mark Miller, Henry Cloud, and most assuredly Patrick Lencioni.

I once heard Doug Mazza, U.S. CEO at Hyundai Motor Company, say, "The best time to fire someone is before you hire them." Here's my take on what he means. If you're truly committed to your business's success, you desperately need skilled individuals overseeing a meticulous hiring process that thoroughly evaluates candidates. By doing so, you'll be capable of discerning top-tier talent from all the other pretenders, avoiding the need to dismiss underperforming employees.

For years, I've seen firsthand how critical it is to build the right team from the outset. I can't stress enough how much easier—and more fulfilling—everything becomes when you have skilled, called, and passionate people around you. It's not just about avoiding the pain of letting someone go; it's about investing in a future that works for everyone involved. When I think back on Doug Mazza's words, I realize they're not just about avoiding missteps; they're about setting a standard. If we're intentional with each hire, we won't just have a team—we'll have the kind of culture and people who propel our vision forward. So, before you make your next hire, ask yourself: Is this person someone I'll be excited to work with tomorrow, next month, and next year? If the answer is "yes," you're already well on your way. In the end, every hire should be seen as a building block that aligns with our vision and values, not merely a temporary solution to a vacancy.

Chapter 1

THE PROBLEM
Why Can't We Stay Here?

"Predictive hiring doesn't create perfect hiring. However, it does significantly increase the likelihood you will hire the right person in the right seat if you're committed to trusting the process."
—Chad Carter

"You Have What You Tolerate!"

How would you describe your hiring process? Would you like to see it become significantly more effective, cutting out mishires and underperforming employees?

If you have a lazy hiring process, it's a one-way ticket to a team full of underperformers and missed opportunities. Every shortcut today sabotages your success tomorrow.

When I begin each of my "Predictive Hiring Model" workshops, I ask participants one question, "Who here follows a specific process when you're filling a hiring need?" Out of approximately 100 participants in each workshop, there might be one or two raised hands. It always astounds me. I've been teaching The Predictive Hiring Model for more than a decade and the responses do not change.

The simple idea of hiring correctly can have a profound impact on creating a high-performance organization. Certainly, you would imagine every new hire results in a fantastic outcome! However, we know that's not the case. Otherwise, this seemingly simple concept would yield results beyond our expectations.

The top reasons leaders make bad hiring decisions are because they compromise and settle for less due to the pressure to perform. The disciplines are not in place to experience excellence in hiring the right person for the job. Clearly, high-performance organizations succeed when leaders establish a rigorous hiring process that they're committed to with a no-compromise approach. Leaders are responsible for the low performance or high performance of every individual within their organization because they reap the results of what they cultivate or tolerate.

High-performance organizations don't fill open positions with whoever walks in the door. Instead, they foster a culture of hiring the best fit for every role because they don't have the luxury of a bad hire! They don't select people and then find themselves trying to convince the new hire to embrace their core values. Instead, high-performance organizations make wise choices to only invite individuals who possess their values and DNA. This ultimately allows the new hire to fulfill their calling, apply their strengths, and find a long-term home.

It Can't Be That Difficult

Why is it that managers take the easy way out, instead of applying excellence in hiring practices?

The reason is simple: Managers believe they're a good judge of character. They say to themselves, "This can't be that difficult." There's this sense of optimism that says, "I'm going to get it right the next time." Unfortunately, that's the definition of insanity- doing the same thing over and over, expecting a different result. Honestly, we know something must change if we're going to experience a different result. If something doesn't change, we allow these mis-hires to wreak havoc on our organizations. They affect the great people we work with, our own personal productivity, and most importantly, the bottom line of our organizations. Somehow, we must stop this.

Solomon, considered by many as the wisest and wealthiest man who ever lived, reminds us in Proverbs 26:10, "Like an archer who wounds at random is he who hires a fool or any passerby." This proverb was written 7,000 years ago and remains so applicable today. This is why it's vitally important to triple the rigor of our hiring process if we intentionally want to become a high-performance organization.

Why can't we stay here? Most would certainly argue that it's the cost. I've read countless books and articles recounting the detrimental effects of bad hiring methods on cost. But, while I wouldn't disagree that the sheer cost is astronomical, the reality is far more devastating than these books and articles suggest.

While the financial losses and missed opportunities are undoubtedly painful, the most significant cost of a bad hire—by far—is the psychological toll on the organization's team members and its leadership. This effect is especially pronounced in small businesses and entrepreneur-led organizations, where leaders are deeply involved in the daily operations. The mental strain of managing underperforming employees saps a manager's mental energy, leading to widespread repercussions on the organization's overall performance. Again, this must stop!

I can't stress this enough: we can't afford to continue implementing poor hiring practices. The ripple effects are too vast and damaging. It's draining our energy, disrupting our team dynamics, and ultimately holding us back from reaching our full potential. Every wrong hire sets us back in ways we can't see immediately—lower morale, higher turnover, and a loss of trust within our team.

The Cycle of Instability and Frustration

I've seen firsthand the cycle of instability and frustration poor hiring can create. It's more than just a financial burden; it's about the time and effort we lose trying to correct these mistakes.

We need to prioritize refining our hiring strategies, not just for the sake of efficiency, but for the future growth and stability of our company. By investing in this vital area, we can build a stronger, more cohesive team that drives us forward and provides a competitive advantage. I'm not talking about a minor tweak. I'm talking about an absolute overhaul of most hiring practices. In fact, some organizations simply need to develop a consistent hiring process after facing the hard reality that they've never had one.

In my workshops, some have voiced that hiring is a "tension to be managed" and not a problem to be solved. This commentary, believed by a number of leaders, is categorically incorrect. This can be solved and I have the data to prove it. The leader who believes this is a "tension to be managed" is most probably overwhelmed by the challenges inherent within hiring and the dynamics of dealing with people. Ultimately, the important thing is to hire in a way that builds the culture within your organization while continually training your leaders to care for your people.

The Predictive Hiring Model will give you a solid roadmap that works. It will provide you with true stories of how others implemented the Model. But it will take significant and consistent effort on your part to remain disciplined in the process.

Looking Back to Move Forward

While every CEO, President of an organization, HR leader, and hiring manager would claim that hiring is a priority…it just isn't so. If it was a priority, their organizations would spend the time to get it right almost every time. That's why you and I are here right now!

Before I spend the majority of our time together in this book explaining "HOW" you need to implement The Predictive Hiring Model, let's look back to move forward by acknowledging and explaining specific problems.

> *"An estimated two-thirds of all hiring decisions are hiring mistakes."*
> —Peter Drucker

Peter Drucker, the father of modern-day management, communicated that the most crucial and most difficult of all decisions were those about hiring and promoting people. He stated, "An estimated two-thirds of all hiring decisions are hiring mistakes."[3] One of the first problems is neglecting to make hiring an imperative priority!

Most managers would estimate that making good hiring decisions holds a 50% probability of success. However, we

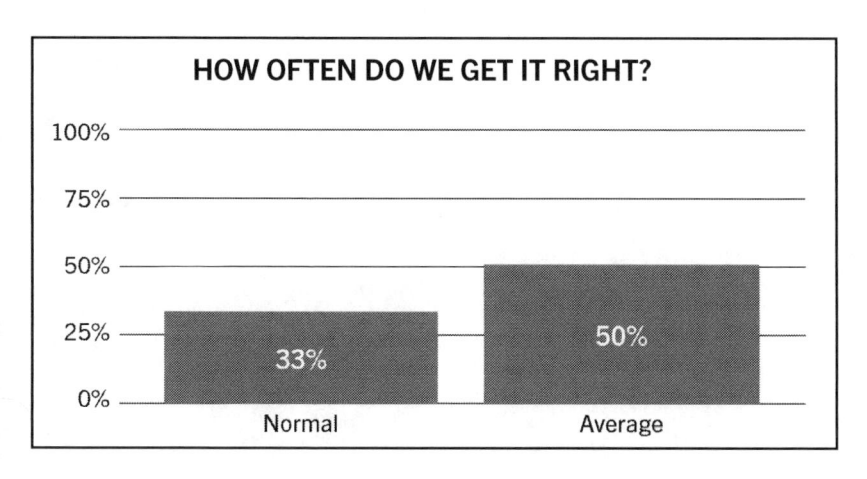

HOW OFTEN DO WE GET IT RIGHT?

Normal	Average
33%	50%

know that a limited number of organizations like Chick-fil-A, Southwest Airlines, and Ritz-Carlton apply a unique formula or strategic hiring process that allows them to achieve results far greater than other organizations. That's why we call them High-Performance Organizations. Chick-fil-A executive Mark Miller states in his book, *Chess Not Checkers,* "If you intend to be a High-Performance Organization, recruit the best, select the best, retain the best, and accept no less."

Secondly, it seems more difficult in today's culture for leaders to take personal responsibility for their own decisions. Yet, in a well-managed organization real leaders step up, accept responsibility, and make the appropriate adjustments.

According to a survey of 444 North American organizations by Right Management, more than two-thirds of organizations report that the cost of hiring mistakes averages two to three times the employee's annual salary. Additionally, the *Harvard Business Review* points out that as much as 80% of employee turnover is due to bad hiring decisions.

Thirdly, Peter Drucker also communicated that often when effective executives find a hiring decision did not produce desired results, they don't conclude that the employee performed poorly, but instead that they themselves made a mistake.

The data seems to support that, while a war for talent wages all around us, the skills and craft necessary to fight the battles of hiring correctly still remain at an all-time low.

Why Is This Happening?

> *"63% of hiring decisions are made within the first 4.3 minutes of an interview."*
> —*USA Today*, Courtesy of Society for Human Resource Management (SHRM)

According to a *Harvard Business Review* study, 90% of successful hires are decided solely upon the interview. Furthermore,

TOP HIRING PITFALLS

1. **Overreliance on Automated Systems.** Dependence on software applications or algorithmic systems for keywords to filter candidates can overlook qualified candidates.

2. **Unstructured Interview Process.** Without a consistent and rigorous interview process, it's difficult to compare candidates fairly.

3. **Applicant Falsifications Elude Hiring Managers.** Hiring managers accept the claims made on resumes at face value when resumes are often nothing more than embellishments of accomplishments with all failures removed. It's like false advertising.

4. **Failure to Define Job Roles Clearly.** Vague job descriptions can attract unqualified candidates when there's no Ideal Candidate Profile.

5. **Lack of Training for Hiring Managers.** Inadequate training can result in inconsistent and biased hiring practices.

6. **Self-Reliance Without Process.** Managers believe they're a good judge of character. They trust their gut. They don't use an orderly process like they would if building a budget.

7. **Hiring Based on Familiar Traits or Relationship.** Hiring based on a particular characteristic the candidate embodies such as character or competence or because they're family.

8. **The Connection Trap.** Hiring managers let their guard down at some point during the interview or the hiring process because they felt a connection with a specific candidate.

9. **Overemphasis on Education and Experience.** Focusing too much on formal qualifications can overlook candidates with practical skills and potential.

10. **Many People Involved in Hiring.** Having too many decision-makers can slow down the process and lead to inconsistent evaluations.

11. **Wrong Interviewers Interviewing.** Having the wrong people interview candidates, instead of evaluating your staff and only having interviewers who possess a High HBA—that's a Hiring Batting Average. I'll explain it later in this book. It's like having a senior executive interview because he or she occupies a role when it would be better to have a fearless individual with a skill or insight in interviewing.

12. **Not Checking References.** Skipping reference checks can mean missing out on vital information about a candidate's past performance.

13. **Bias in the Hiring Process.** Allowing unconscious biases to influence hiring decisions can lead to sameness and numerous missed opportunities.

14. **Rushed Hiring Decisions.** Filling positions quickly without proper evaluation can lead to poor hires. This is immaturity. In a study by CareerBuilder, they found that 43% of the bad hires were caused by feeling the need to rush the hiring decision.

63% of hiring decisions are made within the first 4.3 minutes of an interview (Courtesy of SHRM). This is why it's happening. We have normalized the acceptance of fast hiring with minimal data. This highlights what organizational psychologist Adam Grant refers to as the, "I'm not biased" bias. Think about it: When someone walks out of your office, or off a virtual call, what makes you think it was a good interview? Usually, it's a spark of connection, which happens when you find something in common, not something different.

Speed Kills

Speed, for the sake of speed, will kill your ability to make wise hiring choices. Rushing to fill a position without proper preparation is like accelerating your car into the turn without checking your tires. You'll end up as part of the wall. Consider a Nascar driver—the faster they go, the higher the risk. Yet, they don't shy away from speed. Why? Because they know their car, understand the track, and are prepared for the unexpected.

Later in this book, I'll help you understand the hiring process as your vehicle. I'll demonstrate how you can master this, be prepared for the unpredictable, and increase your speed without indecisiveness or poor quality.

As a Vice President of Human Resources in a healthcare company for several years, I experienced firsthand the intense economic pressures and shortage of qualified healthcare professionals. During one particular interaction with the company President, we were discussing the urgent need to fill Provider roles with either a Nurse Practitioner or a Physician's Assistant. In a moment of frustration, he shouted, "Just get me somebody!"

While I was committed to finding someone who would thrive in our culture and provide exceptional care to our patients, his priorities were clear: he wanted a warm body to drive revenue. Sadly, this approach is all too common in many organizations and is indicative of their lack of priority on a healthy hiring process . . . a process that understands the interconnectedness of all organizational dynamics. Interestingly, after I left the organization, I learned he had been indicted, investigated, and found guilty of Medicare fraud.

> "I would rather endure the pain of not having someone in that position than having the wrong person in that position."
> —Patrick Lencioni, *The Five Dysfunctions of a Team*

I understood the discomfort he felt in maintaining the open position, but I recalled *The New York Times* best-selling author, Patrick Lencioni, saying, "I would rather endure the pain of not having someone in that position than having the wrong person in that position."[4] The temptation to just make a decision is simply unwise because of the ultimate cost to the organization.

I also recall reading Patrick Lencioni's book, *The Motive*, which delves into the motivations behind leadership. It contrasts those driven by self-interest with those who genuinely aim to serve their team, organization, and customers.

My First Impression Was Incorrect

Early in my career, while in Chicago for training, I commuted on the "L," their mass transit system. One particular day, a passenger boarded the L and seemed to be staring at me as he worked his way toward his seat. It was unsettling and made me feel incredibly uncomfortable. Once seated, the passenger fumbled through his backpack and retrieved a notepad. He then held the notepad close to his face as he attempted to read the enormously large handwritten text. I quickly realized the passenger had vision problems and was not staring at me. My first impression was incorrect.

In a professional setting, employers need to be aware of the concept of first-impression bias. First impressions in the interview process can be tremendously misleading. A candidate's interview competency does not always correlate with his or her professional competency. Weak performers may be able to charm interview panels and create a misleading first impression.

Likewise, solid performers may not be accustomed to attending job interviews and his or her nervousness may create a negative impression. This is only one reason we need to establish multiple steps in a rigorous hiring process.

Staying in the Dark

Thomas Edison designed a bulb that was designed to last forever, called the Eternal Light. It was lit the first time on October 22, 1929. The bulb is now located at the Thomas Edison Center at Menlo Park, a small museum near the Edison Memorial Tower in New Jersey. However, in December 1929, a global organization known as the Phoebus Cartel devised a secret plan to increase sales of light bulbs by bringing the average bulb's lifespan down to only 1,000 hours. This began one of the first known examples of planned obsolescence.

What was the planned obsolescence of the light bulb?

There's a light bulb in a fire station in Livermore, California that has been lit for over 100 years. That's right. It's called the "Centennial Light" and it was originally installed in 1901. It has only been turned off a handful of times, yet the filament is still working. How is it possible that a lightbulb can last over 100 years? What's amazing is that making a 100-year filament is actually easy. What's a little tricky is making thin little filaments that are guaranteed to break every year, so that people always need to buy more light bulbs. Imagine this, we could all have lightbulbs that last our entire lives, available for pennies, created with 120-year-old technology. The only problem is big corporations don't want us to have these. They want us to literally stay in the dark. And I think the same goes for the way we hire people in our organizations.

It seems to me that the world profits when you and I stay in the dark and the true causes of turnover—unhealthy, toxic cultures, and low levels of leadership behavior keep our organizations underperforming.

Why Can't We Stay Here?

The status quo is certainly more comfortable, but it yields no results. We experience perpetual pain within our organizations, our teams, and often to ourselves.

Inherent within our current hiring challenges, it is imperative to acknowledge the pressing need for improvement in our processes. Rushed decisions, bias, overreliance on interviews, and neglecting internal candidates, are flaws hindering our ability to attract and retain top talent. Addressing these areas with thoughtful, strategic changes can help us build a more robust, versatile, and effective workforce.

Before you read on, I applaud your commitment to exploring and improving your hiring practices. You wouldn't be reading this if you weren't ready to raise your standards. Let's work together and be intentional about refining these methods. You can develop a hiring process that not only aligns with your values but also creates an environment where both your employees and your organization enjoy a competitive advantage. Let's begin together today!

Chapter 2

THE SOLUTION
The Six Disciplines of Predictive Hiring

"I am convinced that nothing we do is more important than hiring and developing people. At the end of the day, you bet on people not on strategies."
—Lawrence Bossidy

Elizabeth Gilbert wrote in *The Last American Man*, "By the time Eustace Conway was seven years old, he could throw a knife accurately enough that he could nail a chipmunk to a tree." This is something that ninety-nine out of one hundred people couldn't do, but he could because of his constant practice. He made his practice—predictive. That's exactly what I want to do every time I hire someone. I want to be able to predict the right person for the job.

Don't you get tired of hiring someone only to find out they're leaving you just one year later? Can't you literally see all that investment of time, money, and energy going down the drain as you start all over again? It's so exhausting and so frustrating. Yet, we do it every day. Do you want a different result?

Do You Want a Different Result?

This was the question I kept asking myself early in my career. After recently transitioning from working in the music industry in Nashville, TN into a consumer-packaged goods (CPG) company, we were hiring people as fast as we could. The pressure to "Just Get Somebody" was immense. The real indicator of our hiring process was that the back door was larger than the front door. Yes, that's right! Employees were leaving faster than we could bring them in. I wanted to make some needed changes to the process, but the existing leadership team wasn't buying in. We performed nine company acquisitions in nine months and struggled to assimilate the people, processes, and bring in enough new staff to manage the chaos.

Much to my surprise, the executive leadership attempted to buy another company, and instead, the ownership of the target company purchased our business. Looking back, it provided me with 20/20 vision—it was one of the best things that happened in my career. Ultimately, an entirely new executive leadership team came on board. They loved the idea of creating a strategic hiring process that identified various characteristics and competencies within candidates to determine if they would fit within the DNA of our new culture. This concept, while somewhat theoretical to me at the time, just made sense. Back then, I wasn't aware of any experts writing or speaking on the subject of developing hiring processes or streamlining talent acquisition—it felt like the "wild, wild West." Our task was to figure it out on our own.

Upon the purchase of our business, I was blessed to have a new CEO, Doug Cahill. He knew he wanted to build an exceptional culture where team members would not only be attracted to our business but would also want to stay and build something very special together. We did just that!

Doug knew we needed a strong, knowledgeable, experienced HR leader to steer the ship in every way: talent, culture, communications, systems, benefits, payroll, etc. Doug tasked me with hiring my next boss. We utilized one of the largest U.S.-based executive search firms to cultivate the candidate roster. I recall when we narrowed our search down to our final two candidates. Doug sought input from a wide range of team members, and we collectively decided upon Debbie Shecterle.

While I remember many details from those early days in my career, what stands out the most was Debbie as she pressed me daily to improve our hiring process. Moreover, she provided much-needed guidance. This was my introduction to competencies and the cultivation of a hiring process. The process allowed our business to grow revenues from $25 million to $1.3 billion, with several thousand employees. I owe a debt of gratitude to Debbie and Doug for their investment and belief in our ability to successfully bring in hundreds of team members over the decade I served there. Indeed, we built something very special!

While I tweaked and honed this hiring process over the years naming it "The Predictive Hiring Model," its foundation was laid during those years, thanks to the ongoing investment of these two individuals.

"Specifically, The Predictive Hiring Model is a systematic, repeatable process..."

What Is Predictive Hiring?

Predictive hiring leverages data, analytics, assessments, and candidate characteristics to forecast and determine which individuals will be a strong fit for the job role and are likely to succeed in the position. This contrasts with relying solely on traditional methods like resume screening and interviewing. It's a comprehensive, data-driven approach shaped within The Predictive Hiring Model to recruit the best fit for the role.

Candidate characteristics incorporate everything we can discover and know about a candidate before we hire them. These characteristics form the building blocks for the predictions we make about how well a candidate will perform.

Specifically, The Predictive Hiring Model is a systematic, repeatable process that enables hiring managers to make informed decisions and improve the quality of hires.

To be considered "predictive," an organization must transition to a process that:

1. **Standardizes recruitment and hiring procedures across all departments and divisions.** Essentially, this involves creating uniform practices throughout the organization to ensure consistency. Without this consistency, implementing the most effective solutions becomes a challenge.
2. **Clearly define what a "Great Hire" looks like within your organization.** Identify which competencies are crucial and go beyond "The Five Attributes" (which I'll share later in this book and share more deeply in my sister book, *The Five Attributes: Essentials of Hiring*).
3. **Add unbiased and consistent evaluation by adding a layer of objectivity through assessment.** We will delve deeper into this topic in the chapter on Assessment.
4. **Measure candidates based on criteria derived from your high-performing employees.** This is often achieved by developing an "Ideal Candidate Profile." (An example of such a profile is included as a tool in The Predictive Hiring Toolkit at www.PredictiveHiringModel.com.)

Use Predictive Hiring as a Guide

Through extensive research, I've developed and refined The Predictive Hiring Model, and I believe you can greatly benefit from it. Since every organization has its unique needs, when I've led workshops over the years, I've encouraged attendees to identify and implement their top three takeaways within their hiring process, integrating these into The Predictive Hiring Model program. I encourage you to do the same.

If you already have a predictive hiring system in place, make sure to use it to its fullest potential. Remember, it's a tool designed to support hiring managers, not to replace them. These strategies streamline your hiring efforts. They strengthen your ability to make wiser hiring choices and increase your hiring probability to match that of your high-performing team members.

The final hiring decision should always rest with your hiring manager, supported by the HR team, the recruiter, and your senior leadership team. This model and the data provide the necessary insights to make well-informed decisions.

Potential Problems

In my experience with various organizations, I've discovered some common issues that arise with manual approaches that organizations utilize. Here are a few of them:

- **Undefined or Poorly Defined Outcomes:** When success is not clearly defined and articulated, it becomes impossible to predict the factors that will contribute to a successful employee. Without a clear understanding of your goals, achieving them is out of reach.
- **Hiring Manager Assumptions:** Even when outcomes are clearly defined, unless the hiring manager possesses the same characteristics and attributes that align with the other leadership team members, similar outcomes become unattainable.
- **Retention and Use of Data:** Information collected during the hiring process is seldom retained and rarely utilized to assess and determine whether the hypothesized attributes align with desired outcomes.

For more than three decades, I've worked diligently within every human resources discipline. However, the talent recruiting, selection/hiring, and strategic workforce planning are the disciplines I focused on the majority of my career. This laser-focused attention and these efforts enabled me to become a subject matter expert. The truth is... I love hiring people! I love connecting people with a means of supporting themselves. One of my greatest passions is connecting people with their passions

THE RIGHT PEOPLE ON THE BUS

Stanford researcher, teacher, and author, Jim Collins wrote in his groundbreaking book, *Good to Great*, that all decisions should start with "who."

"When we began the research project, we expected to find that the first step in taking a company from good to great would be to set a new direction, a new vision and strategy for the company, and then to get people committed and aligned behind that new direction.

We found something quite the opposite.

The executives who ignited the transformations from good to great did not first figure out where to drive the bus and then get people to take it there. No, they first got the right people on the bus (and the wrong people off the bus) and then figured out where to drive it. They said, in essence, "Look, I don't really know where we should take this bus. But I know this much: If we get the right people on the bus, the right people in the right seats, and the wrong people off the bus, then we'll figure out how to take it someplace great."

The good-to-great leaders understood three simple truths. First, if you begin with "who," rather than "what," you can more easily adapt to a changing world. If people join the bus primarily because of where it is going, what happens if you get ten miles down the road and you need to change direction? You've got a problem. But if people are on the bus because of who else is on the bus, then it's much easier to change direction: "Hey, I got on this bus because of who else is on it; if we need to change direction to be more successful, fine with me." Second, if you have the right people on the bus, the problem of how to motivate and manage people largely goes away. The right people don't need to be tightly managed or fired up; they will be self-motivated by the inner drive to produce the best results and to be part of creating something great. Third, if you have the wrong people, it doesn't matter whether you discover the right direction; you still won't have a great company. Great vision without great people is irrelevant."[5]

and their calling in life. Short of that, hiring becomes merely filling a position with a body causing lazy habits to take over any organization's mission, vision, and values.

Criticism

I made it one of my professional pursuits to create this systematic, repeatable process to be both adaptable and adoptable into any size organization to maximize the quality of hires. When I started to share this model, I received some criticism that the model would only work in large-scale organizations. Now, after more than a decade of sharing this model in live workshops and numerous articles, I've experienced hundreds of follow-ups and testimonials from leaders of every size and scale of organization encouraging me to write about this and share it with you because of the results they achieved.

Some believe this process is just too hard and some believe it's too good to be true. They imagine it can't truly predict the results claimed here. However, that's up to you to decide. In my own experience, I've tested this on the battlefield, and it works like a dream! Yes, it's rigorous. Yes, it can overwhelm you if you let it. But I've never allowed it to do so. It is a dream model for HOW you operate a hiring process and elevate your quality of hire. If you have the courage, you'll also follow my friend, Al Lopus' advice. He assures you in his book, *Road to Flourishing,* you'll create a flourishing culture that retains high caliber talent and lifts your organization to levels you've never experienced previously. His book is a classic read to help ensure your employees thrive.

Whose Job Is It Anyway?

Who is responsible for achieving outstanding results in hiring within your organization? If you're reading this book, it's likely your responsibility or you're at least a key influencer. More specifically, if your organization has a Human Resources lead or team, they should be proficient in this area and excel at the process. Additionally, securing the support of the President & CEO is crucial. I was fortunate to work with senior leadership to obtain their approval for our hiring processes. Without this support, attracting top-tier talent can be challenging. For many in HR aspiring to be involved in the decision-making process, equipping your organization with a predictive tool will accelerate this journey more effectively than any other approach.

While HR may not directly hire employees, their role is to facilitate processes that enable the selection of remarkable talent. As the senior HR officer, I always took it upon myself to oversee this process, making sure our leaders do not become complacent or settle for hires who don't align with the Five Attributes (also known as the Five C's).

Discipline

Discipline is imperative as we discuss the implementation of The Predictive Hiring Model and introduce the Six Disciplines that define its process. The pursuit of discipline has been a lifelong goal of mine. I've found it far easier to wander into lazy habits of mind, body, and spirit than it is to remain focused and productive in vital areas of life. For example, it has taken me ten years to complete this book, though I hoped to release it much sooner.

My oldest son, Joseph, serves in the U.S. Air Force. Through their basic military training (BMT), he was introduced to a new level of discipline. When I visited him in San Antonio, Texas, at the culmination of his training, I found a transformed young man. He stood differently, looked me square in the eye, and spoke with respectful tones. Not to mention, he gained twenty-two pounds of muscle in just a few short months due to the rigorous training and sheer discipline introduced into his life.

Even as I write this, a healthy sense of pride wells up within me, bringing tears to my eyes. There's something remarkable that occurs when we set our sights on a lofty goal that truly demands something from us, stretching and elevating us to a new level of excellence. When we do this, people around us can observe the difference.

I propose to you that introducing discipline allows us to move from aspiring dreams to achieving greatness. Discipline is long obedience in the same direction. However, discipline by itself will not produce great results.

> "Discipline is the soul of an army. It makes small numbers formidable; procures success to the weak and esteem to all."
> —George Washington

"Friedrich Wilhelm August Heinrich Ferdinand Steuben (born Friedrich Wilhelm Ludolf Gerhard Augustin von Steuben; September 17, 1730–November 28, 1794), also referred to as the Baron von Steuben, was a Prussian-born military officer who served as inspector general and Major General of the Continental Army during the American Revolutionary War. He's credited with being one of the fathers of the Continental Army in teaching them the essentials of military drills, tactics, and disciplines. He wrote, *Regulations for the Order and Discipline of the Troops of the United States*, the book that served as the standard United States drill manual until the War of 1812. He served as General George Washington's chief of staff in the final years of the war."[6]

In the beginning of the Continental Army, under the command of General George Washington, rules and regulations were a foreign concept as the majority of the fighting forces were a rag-tag militia of unskilled farmers. This made for a very unorganized military that would cripple easily. Fredrich Von Stueben of Europe noticed these issues and very quickly began teaching a regiment of Washington's army the priority of discipline and drill. Through marching drills and other discipline exercises, this regiment quickly turned from a rag-tag militia to a feared fighting force. They were disbanded after training to become integral parts of other regiments in the same military and taught these skills to the rest of the farmers.

This piece of history is a primary basis why the United States military remains a formidable, dominant force. Discipline is an indispensable skill for all to cultivate. It is crucial in every aspect of life. Although its importance is widely recognized, few take the initiative to develop it, leading to substandard results.

When I worked in Nashville's music industry, I remember a friend who was a songwriter and record producer and who is still very accomplished in his own right. He achieved recognition through several Grammy awards in addition to a Hall of Fame induction and numerous other accolades in the music business.

One morning over breakfast, he shared with me the structured approach he takes to the craft of songwriting. He goes almost every day at a dedicated time to a specific place to write songs. Often, he invites others into this space to collaborate and create timeless masterpieces. While some songs may effortlessly flow from the songwriter, my friend emphasized that most songs are crafted through the discipline of understanding that greatness requires intentional focus.

Given that we spend more time on selecting, managing, and addressing issues related to people than on any other aspect of our jobs, why do managers often overlook the critical need for discipline and focus in hiring decisions? As one of my mentors, Dr. Dewayne Thompson, often says, it should be "Intuitively obvious to the most casual observer." Peter Drucker noted, "No other decisions are so long-lasting in their consequences or so difficult to unmake, than hiring decisions." If your top management or team managers can't grasp this crucial element of management, you might have the wrong people in these vital roles.

It is a truth universally acknowledged that nothing of consequence is gained without sacrifice, struggle, and tremendous discipline.

The Six Disciplines of Predictive Hiring

It is a truth universally acknowledged that nothing of consequence is gained without sacrifice, struggle, and tremendous discipline. No great athlete or musician ever achieved anything remarkable in his or her respective field without immense discipline.

The Predictive Hiring Model mirrors such discipline.

My method has always been to apply the following six disciplines consistently over time. I know these principles work because I've witnessed their success in multiple organizations. By adhering to this healthy process, I've seen the people in these organizations achieve remarkable results. They are the "Olympic gold medals" of my career. We will be addressing each of these principles in future chapters.

THE SIX DISCIPLINES OF PREDICTIVE HIRING

1 Alignment — Involves defining success for the role to ensure clarity about who to hire.

2 Recruitment — Focuses on the strategic data-driven sourcing of candidates.

3 Assessment — Uses structured, evidence-based methods to reduce biases and provide a comprehensive, data-driven evaluation of candidates.

4 Screening — Utilizes predictive analytics to filter and prioritize candidates based on collected assessment data.

5 Offering — Focuses on building rapport, asking a pre-offer question, and presenting offers skillfully.

6 Measured Outcomes — Involves tracking key metrics and making data-driven decisions to refine the hiring process.

Prior to the existence of technology that allowed us to "see" into the ground, people depended on divining rods to find water wells, metals, gemstones, and even missing people. *The Six Disciplines of Predictive Hiring* and *The Five Attributes* point leaders to some vital resources that can benefit them in their hiring process. *The Six Disciplines* and *The Five Attributes* are the diving rods required to assess candidates in The Predictive Hiring Model.

Measured Outcomes Determined This Model "Predictive"?

I never intended to create a "predictive" hiring tool. My goal was simply to address the inefficiencies in hiring and improve the staggering 67% failure rate Peter Drucker declares and most of us experience.

Once I became familiar with the early model's logic, particularly concerning alignment, I began noticing a pattern of success. Hiring managers were more satisfied with their new hires and new hires quickly became productive and engaged. They also stayed with the company, contributing to building a strong team culture. You could feel the energy rising and it felt like we struck gold. It reminded me of my days in the music industry when you would hear certain songs from an artist before their release and instantly knew which ones would be hits. That same feeling was present in our business.

Consequently, I decided it would be prudent to gather feedback from our hiring managers after we brought someone on board. We implemented 90-day and 180-day feedback surveys. While we wanted to understand what we had done right, our primary question was, "If you had it to do over, would you hire this person again?" With a success rate in the 90th percentile, these hiring managers overwhelmingly said, "Yes!" To us, that meant, "It works!"

Let's be honest, it doesn't take long to determine whether we've made a wise hiring decision. We observe the work habits of a new employee, and their ability to think critically, solve problems, and contribute to the team. Conversely, we also notice any questionable behaviors that raise concerns.

Over the years, I've consistently surveyed hiring managers in the organizations I've served, and the statistics remain steady. Additionally, I'll share stories of business owners who have adopted this model and witnessed transformative changes in their businesses.

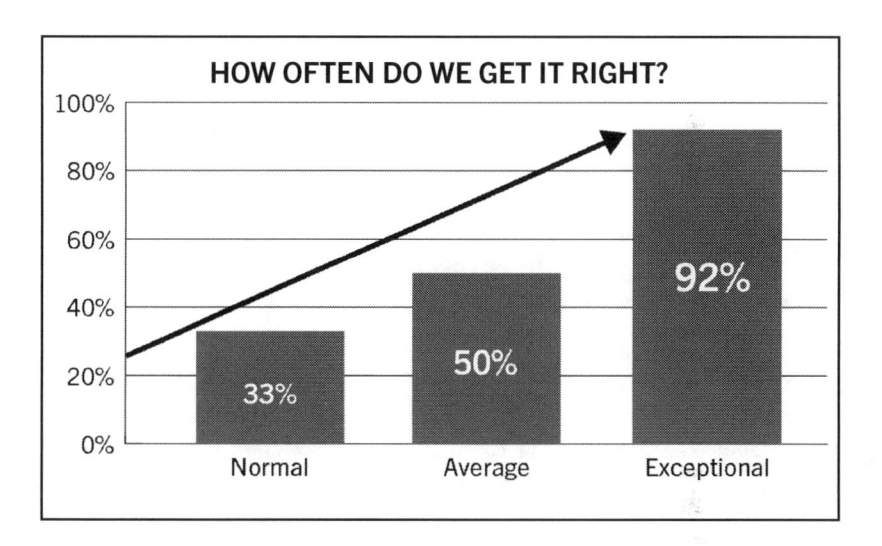

HOW OFTEN DO WE GET IT RIGHT?

Category	Percentage
Normal	33%
Average	50%
Exceptional	92%

Multiplication

Mature leaders hire individuals more talented than themselves. They choose people who can not only utilize their own strengths but also harness the strengths of others. Author and speaker Liz Wiseman refers to these individuals as "Multipliers." They enhance both the organization's culture and its value. One of the greatest contributions a leader can make is to achieve significant results by leveraging the contributions of others. This transforms the leader into a multiplier, rather than just a single contributor, thereby amplifying the efforts of their team through a compounding effect.

Transformative and Remarkable Results

> ### SNAPSHOT IN ACTION
>
> One such story is from Erik Hinson, President of Logistics Worldwide, a warehousing, and logistics company. While attending a conference in Nashville, Erik approached me to tell me his story.
>
> Erik and his Commercial Manager attended one of my Predictive Hiring workshops. He shared that one of the reasons they participated was because, over the previous two years, they had relied on a temp service for candidate recruitment. During that two-year period, they went through two hundred temporary employees.
>
> During the training, they listened as I discussed the importance of slowing down the hiring process and increasing intentionality using The Predictive Hiring Model. After the session, they decided to review the more than 140 behavior-based interview questions I provided in my book, *Essentials of Hiring: The Five Attributes*. They chose their own questions from these examples and developed additional ones based on The Five Attributes. Instead of asking standard interview questions like, "Can you do this or that? OK, you're hired," they began using open-ended, behavior-based interview questions.
>
> Since the training, they measured their hiring results over a two-year period, the same time frame during which they had previously hired two hundred people. Through their newfound intentionality and improved interview questions, focused on The Five Attributes, they only needed to hire twenty people for those same roles. This reduction of 180 people led to significant savings for their bottom line. Additionally, they avoided the emotional and physical stress of constantly hiring and training new staff. They also fostered closer relationships with their employees, as these individuals were more likely to engage within the culture and stay with the company.

I believe you'd agree that the results Logistics Worldwide experienced (described above) were genuine and exciting. However, if you're not convinced or have no intention of actualizing this newfound systematic, repeatable process that yields results, there's no need to waste your time. Yet if you seriously want to master The Predictive Hiring Model, let's embark on this journey together. Learn more about the essence of Alignment in the next chapter.

Chapter 3

ALIGNMENT
Make the Crooked Path Straight

> *"I know exactly who I'm hiring,
> I just haven't met them yet."*
> —Chad Carter

Life-Giving or Life-Threatening

A heartbreaking reality of scoliosis (the curvature of the spine) is the profound impact it can have when left untreated. If severe, it can impair lung function, heart health, and mobility, diminishing overall quality of life. Beyond the physical challenges, it can cause significant emotional distress and affect daily activities. For my nephew who suffers from scoliosis, alignment was critical to his life; without it, scoliosis would have drastically shortened his life.

After thirteen back surgeries, two titanium rods, and forty-six screws, these instruments brought life and healing by being placed as guard rails for growth. These boundaries introduced healing into his body so his heart and other organs wouldn't suffocate from the bowing of his back. I might mention here that he is an amazing young man. Even with all of the pain and tremendous challenges he endured through so many surgeries, I've never heard a complaint pass over his lips.

Like my nephew, our hiring processes also suffer without newfound alignment.

In this chapter, we'll explore the critical role of alignment in hiring which brings teams together to envision who's best to help achieve vision and values. Alignment ensures that every component works together harmoniously, preventing fractures and instability. When everything is aligned, growth isn't just possible—it's inevitable.

> *"If the alignment step is skipped, you sharply decrease the potential of finding high-potential talent by 56%."*
> —Study performed by Watson Wyatt

The First Discipline is Alignment

Alignment is the starting place. Often overlooked because it doesn't seem glamorous, people dismiss it as unnecessary and a waste of time, wanting to jump straight to the bottom line. However, the discipline of addressing alignment is imperative because alignment is the hardest thing to achieve. A study performed by Watson Wyatt revealed, "If the alignment step is skipped, you sharply decrease the potential of finding high-potential talent by 56%."

Think of alignment like tuning a musical instrument. Imagine an orchestra where each musician plays without tuning his or her instrument. The result is cacophony, not harmony. When we tune our instruments, we tune them to a specific reference point, like middle C, to ensure harmony. Similarly, alignment in our efforts means tuning our actions to embody our core values and goals.

Just as musicians discipline themselves to tune their instruments for a cohesive performance, it's necessary for organizations to discipline themselves to align their efforts for success. Without this foundational discipline, achieving true alignment and harmony is nearly impossible.

You need great clarity to know who you're looking for or you introduce unnecessary chaos and risk to the organization.

Alignment is everything! However, if alignment is not a priority within our organizations, it doesn't matter how much work we put into our strategy, structure, processes, and people. The energy we invest will return lackluster results. The ultimate price is dysfunction which includes team disengagement, lost customers, high turnover, and diminishing returns. However, leaders who slow everything down and insist (with a no compromise approach) on clarity for alignment in every channel, experience a focus that yields trust, peace, and confidence in their leadership decisions.

Alignment is always a first step and a continual process to evaluate whether you are still heading in the right direction. Imagine working in an organization where every employee, from top leadership to the new hire, all share a common passion, heart, and understanding for the organization. Imagine getting up every morning and believing that you make a significant difference in the daily operations of your organization. You make that difference because you utilize your strengths, voice, and ideas which leaders hear. This enables you to make contributions that generate the change or profits your organization requires to remain relevant. That's what you need when you hire and retain a new employee.

Of course, alignment must come from within your own ranks prior to hiring. But why is alignment so hard to achieve? It appears there are literal forces within our organizations that are competing as if there is an enemy within causing confusion and inefficiency. Otherwise, how could well-meaning people of the same organization, who share a common purpose and vision, dispense such damage on one another? I believe it's grounded in the old adage, "We have met the enemy, and he is us."[7]

Without an internal compass and the appropriate processes in place for our hiring needs, we literally bring damage to our front door, our organizations are harmed because we lack discipline, and in some cases, any sense of direction. We keep trying a new direction, idea, or program, desperately hoping this one will work, without any proven methods that guarantee we're headed in the right direction. Shocking, but true.

Isn't this the same thing that's happening in our global economy? We know without question to be fiscally responsible; we must spend less than we take into our coffers. Yet, within our legislative and executive branches of the United States government, we continually raise the debt ceiling, completely aware that these perpetual decisions harm our nation and many others. This is not a political statement, but simply recognition of fiscal responsibility.

Can We Make the Hard Decision?

We need to make a significant course adjustment and insist that we re-engineer our hiring process within our organizations. Hiring correctly should literally be one of the leading philosophies within our organization to affect change and achieve results. Nothing new or exciting will happen within our organization until we are as passionate about hiring the right people as we are about our bottom-line profits. People will always come before profits because people drive our profits through innovation, or they drive our internal dysfunction. It's our choice!

There is one thing that can totally ruin a great hire—the quality of management. Of course, this book isn't about the quality of management. Over the years, I've learned that we can create a tremendous organizational culture with every opportunity for people and the organization to succeed. However, if the manager doesn't possess the required competence for their staff to succeed, employees will leave the organization. People join organizations based on culture but leave due to poor managers.

If we drive to alignment and ultimately achieve it in our people processes, we link the hiring of competent, called, and passionate people with the other tenets of organizational effectiveness—strategy, structure, and processes.

What You Reward Gets Repeated

> ### SNAPSHOT IN ACTION
>
> I recently heard Robert Henderson, owner of an auto service center that specializes in vehicle handling, suspension, steering, and braking of all types of consumer and commercial vehicles explain how a slight misalignment caused their business to experience large consequences. Robert's thoughts on alignment applies to every business and definitely to our hiring processes. "We look at alignment from the standpoint of what happens to that alignment when it's out in the real world ... when you've got ruts, passing trucks, and uneven road conditions ... all these forces working against you. The same thing is true in our businesses. Most of the time things are going smoothly, but what happens when you have a cash flow problem or personnel problems? Can you keep everything aligned under pressure? We found our own company out of alignment as we grew. We went from a service organization to a parts and wholesale company. While part of our staff was rewarded for sending customers to another dealership, other staff members were rewarded for bringing in new customers.
>
> "That created a misalignment in our company. We had internal, unhealthy competition going on. So, we reorganized under this motto, One Company – One Team – One Culture. Now the question is 'What's best for the customer?' If it's best for us to send the customer somewhere else, we do that. If it's best for them to come to us, we let them know that. We created a reward system around this which helped bring our company back into alignment."[8]
>
> Robert's story is an excellent description of leading an organization into alignment.

Here is another example. My friend was attempting to rush out of his home one day to attend a business meeting, but when he pressed the garage door opener, nothing happened. He had hit this garage door opener button a thousand times before and everything functioned properly. However, this time ... nothing happened. He couldn't even get the car out of the garage, so he had to call and reschedule the meeting, while also calling the garage door technician.

Fortunately, he called a technician with integrity. The gentleman asked him to go check out the garage door sensors at the bottom of each side of the door. He asked him, "Are they aligned?" "Have they gotten knocked in a different direction?" If they aren't aligned, then the beam is interrupted, and the door simply won't work properly. All my friend needed to do was reach down and re-adjust the beam so that the sensors were aligned. It didn't cost him anything and a simple adjustment allowed the door to function correctly.

Remember, when alignment exists everything works smoothly. But when we are even one degree off, it creates dysfunction and the little things that we often enjoy that enhance our businesses and relationships, well, they're just off!

Business owners, managers, and HR leaders who refuse to align their values, relationships, processes, and even their relationship with God, will face closed doors and blocked dreams. When any of these are out of alignment, our decisions and direction are skewed, and we end up in a place where we never dreamed we'd land. It's all about alignment. You cannot succeed without it![9]

Building Trust

We build alignment with each other by building trust. Trust is the cornerstone of any successful hiring process. When employees recognize the hiring process as thorough, fair, and well-executed, it reinforces their belief in the organization's leadership and values. Trust in hiring isn't only about choosing the right candidates; it's also about demonstrating a commitment to the team's well-being and the company's long-term success.

When hiring is handled with care and precision, employees feel valued and confident that their colleagues are selected for their competencies and cultural alignment. This trust boosts morale, fosters a sense of security, and enhances team cohesion.

Conversely, when hiring is inconsistent or haphazard, it signals a lack of diligence and can make employees question the stability and direction of the organization.

JPL Cares, a commercial landscaping company, faced severe turnover and instability that puzzled the company's president and founder, Jim Lynch. Eventually, Jim uncovered an unsettling truth. "At the time, my eyes were off the ball. Trust didn't even cross my mind," he explains. "I was really bamboozled when everything happened the way it did because I did feel like I could trust [this employee]. I started feeling like I was losing trust with my staff. They didn't trust me because I wasn't keeping my eye on the ball, and I allowed them to suffer under the leadership of this [individual]. I pulled the company together and told them that I made a mistake with this person and that I was sorry. Through this whole mess, I was left without the right leadership, team members left, and I had no money. I believe this happened to help make me the kind of leader who would build processes and structures for the way we hire people. Now we trust but also verify so we have accountability. We validate whether someone is trustworthy and competent to do the job. The business is better than ever now because of these processes."

Trust in hiring is not just about filling roles but also about nurturing a culture of mutual respect and shared purpose. This trust, once established, propels our organizations forward, encouraging loyalty, engagement, and collective success.

What if we reimagined hiring as a foundational opportunity for deep collaboration?

What Alignment Is and Is Not

Hiring is not simply about filling a vacancy, it's also about finding the right person who will help shape the future of the organization. The decision to hire a new employee is an opportunity to realign, refocus, and recalibrate the entire team's direction.

Alignment is tricky. It's not just about matching skills to a role; it's about ensuring that every new hire understands, embodies, and contributes to the core values that drive your mission. In a world where talent is abundant, but alignment is rare, how do we ensure that our hiring decisions reflect the true essence of what we need—today and tomorrow?

For most organizations, hiring is still seen as a transactional process—a step to fill a role, check a box, or meet a quota. What if we reimagined hiring as a foundational opportunity for deep collaboration? What if, instead of simply deciding 'who fits,' we focused on 'who will make us better'? It's easy to get lost in resumes and qualifications, to over-index on past experience or technical proficiency. But those things alone won't guarantee success. The real magic lies in finding someone who brings not only the right skills but the right mindset, the right approach to problem-solving, and most importantly, the right values that align with the team's culture and the company's mission.

This alignment is the invisible thread that weaves together high-performing teams. It's what makes communication smoother, collaboration more efficient, and long-term goals achievable. But achieving alignment in hiring is no small feat—it requires trust, transparency, and a deliberate, thoughtful approach from everyone involved in the process. When teams collaborate on hiring, they aren't just vetting candidates; they're coming together to ensure that this decision is the best one for the entire organization's evolution.

To truly reimagine your hiring process by creating actionable steps, I encourage you to frame the beginning of the hiring process as a moment of intentional alignment. Here's how you could break it down.

Where Do We Start?

The journey toward alignment in hiring begins not with the candidates, but with the team itself. Before even looking at resumes, before drafting a job description, the first step is to clarify—internally—what you truly need. Not just in terms of skills or qualifications, but in terms of values, culture, and team dynamics. What kind of energy, mindset, and drive will complement the strengths of the current team? What gaps are you aiming to fill, not just for today, but for the organization's future direction in the next few years?

This is where collaboration begins. Too often, the hiring process is "siloed." One department writes the job description, another conducts interviews, and the hiring decision comes down to just a few voices. But when teams collaborate deeply from the outset they can articulate the bigger picture: How will this hire impact the team dynamic? Will this person challenge us to grow or will they simply 'fit in'? What does success look like for him or her in this role, and how will that success contribute to our collective mission?

Achieving alignment within the team means having honest conversations about what everyone needs. This isn't only about agreeing on the technical requirements of the role. This is also about having a shared vision that defines what success looks like and ensures everyone functions in unity when it comes to the broader company goals. Whether it's leadership, communication style, or problem-solving approach, the hiring process must be rooted in understanding these deeper, sometimes intangible qualities.

So, the first step is to come together as a team—beyond the hiring manager—and have a candid conversation about these questions. Only then can you begin the work of defining exactly what you're looking for in a candidate and how that aligns with the organization's current needs and future aspirations.

This is where the real work of "alignment" begins: getting the hiring team to agree about what matters most beyond just skills or experience. By engaging in this reflective process first, teams ensure that the entire hiring effort is intentional, harmonious, and rooted in a shared vision of success. Once this internal alignment is established, you can begin crafting a job description, screening candidates, and conducting interviews—all with a clearer sense of purpose and direction.

When alignment isn't achieved, often a divide emerges late in the hiring process. Differing opinions about the new hire surface and derail the entire process. Aligning hiring managers to agree on a job requisition and an Ideal Candidate Profile before advertising is crucial for a successful hiring process. Here are some steps to achieve that alignment:

1. **Alignment Kickoff**: Gather the hiring manager and key stakeholders to discuss the role. Ensure agreement around the job's value to the organization and how it fits into the broader long-term goals.

2. **Job Requisition**: The job requisition initiates the hiring process and ensures that all stakeholders are aligned and agree concerning requirements and expectations for the new role. It also allows for vital upfront discussions involving details like compensation range for the position and whether relocation is a component of the role. Skipping these initial conversations can lead to fragmented "popcorn discussions" with various key stakeholders throughout the process, resulting in missed details. For an example, please refer to The Predictive Hiring Toolkit at www.PredictiveHiringModel.com.

3. **Clearly Defined Job Blueprint**: Collaboratively create a detailed job description that outlines the responsibilities, required skills, qualifications, and expectations for the role. Make sure the hiring manager and key stakeholders agree on these criteria.

4. **Ideal Candidate Profile**: Develop an Ideal Candidate Profile that highlights not just the skills and experience needed, but also the soft skills, cultural fit, and potential for growth within the organization. This helps create a unified vision of the team's optimal candidate.

ALIGNMENT: Make the Crooked Path Straight | 37

5. **Leveraged Data Insights**: Review relevant data to create benchmarks, including performance metrics from former employees in similar roles, industry benchmarks, and market trends. This helps set realistic expectations and ensures a unified understanding of what defines a strong candidate.

6. **Agreed Upon Interview Process**: Establish and agree on the interview stages. Who will be involved at each stage? What structures will be used for interviews (panel interviews, individual interviews, etc.)? What key behavior-based questions or competencies will hiring managers use to assess the candidates? This ensures a consistent and fair evaluation process.

7. **Communication Tools**: Utilize collaborative tools that include shared documents, project management software, or dedicated HR platforms to keep everyone on the same page throughout the hiring process. Regular updates and open communication channels ensure that all team members are informed, aligned, and able to address any issues or changes promptly.

8. **Feedback Loop**: Establish a process for gathering and integrating feedback from the hiring manager and key stakeholders throughout the process. This helps to continuously help refine the hiring strategy and maintain alignment.

Taking these steps will help ensure the hiring manager and key stakeholders agree, resulting in a more effective and streamlined hiring process.

Slow Down to Speed Up

As mentioned earlier, the job requisition initiates the hiring process and provides final approval for the position. It is imperative to obtain the written approval of the functional senior executive for the division.

Early in my career, I was unaware of such an approval process for the headcount. In one situation, a hiring manager assured me that the President had approved the headcount. Trusting his word, I proceeded. After a few weeks in the hiring process, the company President appeared in my office, questioning why we were moving forward with this position. When I recounted the exchange, he became quite upset. Sincerely, I don't believe anyone lied to me. I simply believe there was a miscommunication between the President and the hiring manager.

It didn't take long to realize the necessity of a job requisition. Introducing this step into the process ensured that I never face this type of situation again. I've found that by taking the time to follow these alignment steps, my team and I can accelerate through other parts of The Predictive Hiring Model seamlessly. However, without these essential guiding documents, we lose our direction, tools, and reference points, resulting in chaos and inefficiency—certainly not an ideal situation.

Reflecting on these experiences, I learned that taking the time to establish proper procedures and gain necessary approvals is crucial. It may seem like a slow start, but this disciplined approach allows for a smoother, faster process in the long run. By "slowing down to speed up," we set the stage for a more efficient, effective hiring process that prevents costly mistakes and misunderstandings. This thoughtful approach drives true success and alignment within the organization causing new hires to embrace their calling. In the end, if you implement the alignment step for The Predictive Hiring Model, you'll also say, "I know exactly who I'm hiring, I just haven't met them yet."

Chapter 4

RECRUITMENT
Attracting the Right People

"The team with the best players wins."
—Jack Welch

It's All About "Who"

This might sound unconventional, but I truly believe attracting the right people into your organization can be one of the most exciting adventures you experience. I'm about to do everything possible to prove this reality to you.

Several years ago, when I was about to address a large group of leaders on the subject of hiring, a bookseller introduced herself to me. She quickly blurted out how boring she found my topic, stating, "I bring boxes of books about hiring to this convention every year, only to box them up and send them back to the publishers." Talk about demotivating! It was obvious to me that no one clearly stated why this critical competency of hiring is such a necessary skill to develop.

After her attempt to squelch my enthusiasm, I still had to ascend the stairs and speak to this group of leaders. I'm pleased to say that later that same day, she tracked me down at the conference and exclaimed, "I've never heard anyone communicate the importance of hiring so effectively and passionately. You've convinced me that I need to give greater focus to this critical area for leaders." I smiled, thanked her, and felt I made a difference in at least one person's perspective that day.

In Jim Collins' landmark book, *Good to Great*, he emphasizes that truly great organizations prioritize the right people above all else. They don't place sales, marketing, finance, or even their strategy at the top of the list. It's the people who come first. Attracting the right talent is serious business, requiring a rigorous process to identify suitable candidates and thoughtful leadership to engage and retain them.

As Collins puts it, "First who, then what." With the right people "on the bus" many common human resource issues never arise. These individuals are self-motivated, with uncommon passion and focus, and willingly contribute their discretionary energy. This is not the case with someone who is a poor fit.

My favorite insight from Collins is the simple truth that "great vision without great people is irrelevant." Without the right team, the direction of the bus won't matter because you'll suffer the lost opportunity … the cost of hiring the wrong people. What a shame.

Ninety Percent of the Equation

> "Hiring the right people is 90% of the equation at Chick-fil-A."
> —Mark Miller

While attending a conference several years ago, I listened to Chick-fil-A's Vice President for Organizational Effectiveness, Mark Miller, say, "Hiring the right people is 90% of the equation at Chick-fil-A." To me, that was an astounding statistic.

However, I agree with him. You can't motivate the *wrong* person to make the *right* decision.

Upon returning home to Nashville, I interviewed four Chick-fil-A Owner/Operators to learn more about their hiring practices. Have you ever noticed that Chick-fil-A employees have brighter eyes, more smiling faces, and greater alertness compared to staff at other local quick-service restaurants? It certainly appears that way to me. Well, there's a reason for that.

> ## SNAPSHOT IN ACTION
> Chick-fil-A has developed a smart talent pipeline strategy. They distribute "Chick-fil-A One Rewards Cards" that double as vouchers for free Chick-fil-A sandwiches to local high school principals. Principals can then give the vouchers to teachers to reward their best students. As these top-performing students return the vouchers to the store and meet the Owner/Operator, Chick-fil-A identifies them as ideal candidates for employment. This clever approach helps them discover and attract talented individuals from the community. This is sheer genius! This is exactly what you need to do—determine where your ideal candidates live, determine how you can approach them, and then attract them to your organization.

The Second Discipline Is Recruitment

Recruitment is the second discipline within The Predictive Hiring Model. I compare recruitment to a treasure hunt for hidden gems to join your organization. You are the Indiana Jones of this story. You take an exhilarating journey uncovering exceptional talent, engaging them with compelling stories of your company's vision, and inviting them to become part of a transformative adventure. This process is not just about filling vacancies; instead, it's about crafting a future where innovative ideas and passionate people come together to create something remarkable. Recruitment is the fine art of connecting with the right individuals whose unique skills and values align with your organization's mission, setting the stage for groundbreaking achievements and unparalleled success.

To achieve this, we build the employment brand, define our employee value proposition, and mine the talent pipeline as though we were digging for gold. Create a strong employer brand that resonates with the values and aspirations of your ideal candidates and showcase why your organization is the best place for them to grow and thrive. You don't want to attract everyone to your job opening. Instead, you want to attract the right person to your job opening with The Five Attributes. We'll unfold those attributes later when we discuss the Screening Discipline.

Employee Value Proposition: Tailored Just For You

Building a strong employment brand begins with creating a clear and compelling employee value proposition (EVP) that defines what makes your organization a unique workplace. The EVP serves as the foundation for attracting, engaging, and retaining top talent by communicating the benefits, opportunities, and culture that sets your organization apart. Once you establish the EVP, it's crucial to weave it into every touchpoint of the candidate and employee experience, from recruiting advertisements to onboarding and internal development. Simultaneously, investing in developing a robust talent pipeline ensures that your organization is not only filling immediate roles but also cultivating future leaders. This requires a proactive approach, leveraging data, relationships, and strategic partnerships to consistently engage high-potential individuals before the need arises. Some have said this can only be implemented at large companies. That's just not true!

I've worked at and consulted with many small organizations, all the while utilizing this approach with tremendous success. Here's an outstanding employee value proposition (EVP) tailored for a small to mid-sized company that emphasizes its unique strengths and opportunities.

Join ABC Company: Where Your Growth Fuels Our Growth

At ABC Company, our people are our greatest asset. As a small to mid-sized company, your contributions are valued and celebrated. Here's what makes us special:

1. Close-Knit Community
   - *Collaborative Culture:* Work where ideas thrive, and every voice matters.
   - *Supportive Team:* Build meaningful relationships with direct access to leadership.
   - *Recognition:* Your achievements are celebrated through shoutouts, feedback, and awards.

2. Real Impact and Growth
   - *Meaningful Work:* Your efforts drive real change and tangible results.
   - *Career Development:* Grow with personalized plans, mentorship, and learning opportunities.
   - *Empowerment:* Innovate and shape your role with autonomy.

3. Flexibility and Well-Being
   - *Work-Life Balance:* Enjoy flexible hours and remote options to fit your life.
   - *Wellness Programs:* Comprehensive benefits for your physical and mental health.
   - *Family-Friendly Policies:* Generous leave, childcare support, and family-inclusive events.

4. Innovation and Creativity
   - *Challenging Projects:* Engage in work that inspires creativity and drives progress.
   - *Empowered Decisions:* Take ownership and make an impact.
   - *Open Ideas:* Share feedback freely in a judgment-free zone.

5. Purpose and Values
   - *Mission-Driven:* Join a team passionate about making a positive impact.
   - *Ethical and Sustainable:* Work with integrity toward a greater purpose.

ABC Company offers more than a job—we offer a place where you can bring your whole self to thrive, grow, and make a meaningful difference. Join us to be part of a team where your work matters, and your well-being is a priority.

Here are a few inspiring stories from organizations that have successfully lived out their employee value proposition (EVP):

- **Patagonia:** *Environmental Stewardship.* Patagonia, an outdoor clothing company, has an EVP centered around environmental stewardship and sustainability. Their commitment to ethical practices and reducing their environmental impact resonates with employees who share these values. Patagonia offers programs like "Worn Wear," which encourages customers to repair and reuse their products, and provides grants to environmental organizations. This alignment of values creates a dedicated and passionate workforce.

- **Zappos:** *Delivering Happiness.* Zappos, an online shoe and clothing retailer, is known for its unique EVP of "Delivering Happiness." Their focus on customer service and employee happiness creates a highly engaged and motivated workforce. Zappos offers a range of benefits, including a 365-day return policy, a fun and inclusive work environment, and opportunities for personal and professional growth. This approach has resulted in high employee satisfaction and customer loyalty.

- **Chick-fil-A:** *Care, Community, and Commitment*: Chick-fil-A emphasizes creating a culture where employees feel valued, supported, and empowered to grow personally and professionally. Chick-fil-A is committed to treating everyone with honor, dignity, and respect. They offer a full range of benefits to support their employees' well-being and career development.

My youngest son, Stephen, began his journey at our local Chick-fil-A in Franklin, Tennessee, as a Team Member. With an unwavering positive attitude and a dedication to making others feel welcomed and valued, Stephen quickly became an integral part of the team. Over his ten-year tenure, his recognized hard work and commitment caused the Owner/Operator to promote him to Team Trainer, then Team Leader, then Shift Leader, and eventually to Catering Director.

Even while pursuing his graduate studies at St. John's University in Queens, New York, Stephen continued to contribute remotely. His Owner/Operator entrusted him with social media and digital marketing projects, which Stephen managed with diligence, significantly enhancing their online presence. Moreover, he was awarded the Chick-fil-A Scholarship for all four years of his undergraduate education.

Stephen's story is a testament to Chick-fil-A's nurturing culture of care and support. It exemplifies how the company not only fosters growth and development within its employees but also prepares them for future outside success.

Creating An Emotional Connection

Perfecting the hiring process is crucial, but it's equally important to impact the hearts and minds of people as you journey together. Building an emotional connection during recruitment goes beyond merely evaluating qualifications; it's about genuinely understanding and appreciating each candidate's unique story and aspirations.

While serving as the VP of Human Resources for a veterinary corporation, I was tasked with hiring a new Chief Operating Officer who had earned a Doctor of Veterinary Medicine (DVM), a Master of Business Administration (MBA), led a veterinary clinic/hospital, and served at least two years on the operations leadership team for a veterinary healthcare corporation.

This was like finding a needle in a haystack! We wondered if we could attract such an individual to our business. After extensive research, we discovered that only four individuals in the United States held the requisite qualifications. We reached out to each candidate, and eventually, we narrowed it down to one outstanding individual who also possessed The Five Attributes. Over three months my team and I walked him through our rigorous hiring process. It culminated in his final visit to our corporate offices. As we listened, we learned through conversations that he, his wife, and their three-year-old daughter wanted to visit Nashville to explore real estate for their future home.

When they arrived, my Director of Human Resources, Claire Moye, had prepared a thoughtful basket for them, focusing on their daughter. It included drinks, snacks for their two-day visit, coloring books, crayons, specific snacks for a three-year-old, and a teddy bear. We got down on the floor with their daughter to give her the bear before they left our offices to tour homes with a hand-selected real estate representative. As Claire connected with their daughter, I saw tears of appreciation in the eyes of our hopeful candidate and his wife. Later, when I spoke with the candidate just before he accepted our job offer, he remarked that he had never experienced such attention to detail and inclusion of family members in the hiring process. We were elated to welcome him and his family into the future plans for our veterinary healthcare corporation.

Reflecting on this experience, I learned a valuable lesson. While the hiring process is vitally important, creating an emotional connection with the candidate's spouse and family is equally crucial, as the entire family is supported by the job the candidate will take. By embracing this comprehensive approach, we not only secured an exceptional Chief Operating Officer but also strengthened our organization's bond with an entire family, ensuring a foundation of trust, support, and mutual commitment that would drive our shared success.

Recruitment as a Strategic Imperative

Recruitment. The mere mention of the word often conjures images of endless resumes, interviews, and the painstaking process of finding that perfect candidate. But what if recruitment could be something more? What if it could become a transformative experience that not only reveals the right people but also strengthens and enhances the very fabric of your organization? Welcome to the world of recruitment excellence, where the focus isn't just on filling positions, but on building a cohesive, high-performing team that embodies the organizational values and mission.

Recruiting is not merely a function of human resources; it is a strategic imperative with buy-in from senior leadership. Great organizations, regardless of size, understand that the right people are the fuel for achieving their dreams. They approach recruitment with the same rigor and discipline they apply to their core business strategies.

Let's take a look at external recruiting first.

For years, HR professionals and organizational leaders often adopted a "Farmer" approach to recruiting. There's nothing inherently wrong with being a farmer, but let's see if this approach holds up today given the current challenges in the job market.

The Farmer Approach

Farmers plant seeds through singular job ads on platforms like LinkedIn, CareerBuilder, or Indeed. They diligently follow hiring rules and regulations, believing that when they sow the seed, a crop will eventually grow. However, the term "toxic" describes the current climate within our ecosystem: there are fewer job candidates available, the business environment is not always friendly, and economic inflation is often out of control.

In this scenario, waiting for the seeds to grow isn't as reliable as it once was. The passive approach of sowing and waiting doesn't yield the results needed in today's competitive job market. This brings us to a more dynamic and proactive model.

> *Do everything you did as a farmer and add to your toolkit the proactive strategies of a hunter.*

The Hunter Approach

Imagine recruiting as if you were a hunter. Do everything you did as a farmer and add to your toolkit the proactive strategies of a hunter.

Hunters prepare meticulously before they even go hunting. They gather the appropriate weapon, ammunition, clothing, and plan their route. Similarly, you'll need to prepare a model of the ideal candidate for each role by analyzing your current successful employees. Why have they been successful? How can you replicate their success? What competencies and characteristics have contributed to their fruitfulness?

Once you have this model, you set the right bait to attract the right candidates. This involves creating compelling job descriptions and employer branding that attracts the ideal talent. Initiate conversations and take an ACTIVE APPROACH rather than a PASSIVE one.

Networking and Engagement

Three aspects of recruitment will enhance your pursuit for quality candidates, the first being networking and engagement. Regardless of the size of the organization, you can't sit and wait for candidates to come to you. It is important to navigate through a networking maze, asking many people for referrals, and sending out emails to your network. Your sphere of influence should include everyone you respect professionally. And don't forget those you're close to in your church, synagogue, and community. Create a counsel that will email you potential candidates for job openings. Some years ago, I created a list of more than two hundred people I know and respect within my network. I call them the "Council of 200". I email them when

I'm recruiting for about any role. I'm always amazed how these folks come to my aid with great names and talent!

The divergent paths of the farmer and the hunter highlight a fundamental shift in recruitment strategies. The farmer's approach, reliant on patience and passivity, struggles in the face of a shrinking talent pool and a competitive market. The hunter's approach, characterized by proactivity and engagement, thrives by actively seeking and attracting top talent.

By combining the farmer's diligence with the hunter's proactive strategies, you can cultivate a robust talent pipeline even in a challenging job market. This dual approach ensures you do not wait for talent but instead actively seek it out, engaging with potential candidates, and bringing them into your organization. The future of recruitment lies in the balance of these two approaches.

Can you see the difference?

FARMER *We were trained to be farmers.*	**HUNTER** *This is who we need to become.*
• Plant Seed through a Job Ad	• Prepare Yourself
• Follow Rules/Regulations	• Create Model of Ideal Candidate for each Role
• We Wait	• Initiate Conversations
• Depends on Market Conditions	• Set the Right Bait
• Bottomline: We Expect Crop	• Go Find Them!

Building a Talent Pipeline

A second proactive approach to recruitment involves building a talent pipeline—a pool of qualified candidates who are interested in your organization and ready to step into roles as they become available. A talent pipeline reduces time-to-hire and ensures you have access to top talent when you need it. How do you develop this pipeline?

Start by identifying key roles within your organization that are critical to its success. These are the roles causing you to initiate and build a talent pipeline. Next, implement the first strategy of recruitment above… engage with potential candidates through networking events, industry conferences, and social media. Create a talent community by offering valuable content such as industry insights, career advice, and company updates. This keeps potential candidates interested in your organization.

Nurture relationships with candidates in your talent pipeline through regular communication. Provide job opening updates, invite them to company events, and share news about your organization's achievements. When a suitable role becomes available, you have a ready pool of qualified candidates who are already familiar with your organization and excited about the opportunity. (I also retain a "rainy day" file. This includes the resumes and contact information for all ideal candidates I'm currently interested in bringing into my organization.)

When I worked at one of Nashville's renowned record companies, I met Michelle Box through our hiring process. From the outset, it was clear that Michelle embodied our organization's core values and The Five Attributes. What stood out was her meticulous nature; Michelle was determined to find the perfect fit in every aspect. Coming from a reputable company, she wasn't willing to make a move unless every "i" was dotted and every "t" was crossed. Honestly, I couldn't blame her.

Our discussions spanned several different positions over many months. Michelle's exacting standards and our mutual quest for the perfect fit meant that each role was carefully considered. It wasn't until the fourth position—an influential project management role—did we finally succeed in bringing her on board. The wait was undeniably worth it. Michelle became an invaluable asset to the team, exemplifying dedication, and excellence in her new role. Her story is a testament to the importance of persistence and the pursuit of the right fit in creating a truly remarkable team.

Below is a collection of valuable resources to help you begin internal and external recruiting; however, this list is by no means exhaustive.

TALENT PIPELINE: *Recruitment*

Internal Pipeline

- Organization's Intranet
- Employee Referral Program
- Rainy Day File
- Internal Job Postings
- Succession Planning
- Targeted International Options within our Organization
- Email your Colleagues & Connections: Council of 200

External Pipeline

- Social Media Marketing
- LinkedIn, Instagram, FB, YouTube
- Colleges & Universities
- Job Boards: Indeed, CareerBuilder, Slack, Dice
- Recruitment Agencies
- Professional Associations
- Alumni Networks & Internships
- Community Places of Worship

The Power of Employee Referrals

Employee referrals are one of the most effective sources of quality hires and the third initiative for retention. Employees understand your culture and can identify candidates who are a good fit. Referred candidates are often more engaged, perform better, and have higher retention rates.

To harness the power of employee referrals, create a structured referral program with clear guidelines and incentives. Communicate the benefits of the referral program to employees and encourage them to participate. Provide tools and resources to make it easy for employees to refer candidates, such as templates for referral emails and social media posts.

Recognize and reward employees who make successful referrals. This reinforces the value of the referral program and motivates employees to continue participating. Celebrate referral hires publicly to highlight the program's success and encourage further engagement.

If you choose to incentivize your employees through a referral program, ensure the rewards truly resonate with them. For instance, one company offered to cover an employee's mortgage or rent for an entire month if their referral was hired and stayed for at least six months. They then asked the employee to take a family photo in front of their home for internal marketing purposes. By providing meaningful incentives, you significantly engage your employees in the process. Without substantial rewards, your employee referral program may fail to make a significant impact. If you think this might be too expensive, consider the cost of hiring an external recruiter. It could shift your perspective.

Create an Attractive Employer Brand

Think about your favorite brand. What makes it stand out? The same principles apply when creating an attractive employer brand for your organization. It's not just about posting job openings—it's about telling a story that sets you apart and resonates with potential candidates.

Imagine your employer brand as a living, breathing entity. It's the collective perception of what it's like to work at your company, encompassing your culture, values, work environment, and employee value proposition. It's the magnet that draws talent to you, differentiating your organization in a crowded job market.

Begin with introspection. What makes your company unique? Is it your commitment to innovation, your family-like atmosphere, or perhaps your dedication to social responsibility?

Understanding what sets you apart is crucial. Engage with your current employees because their experiences and perceptions provide a gold mine of insight. Their stories and feedback will help craft an authentic, compelling narrative about your organization.

Once you've defined your brand, it's time to broadcast it. Consistency is key. Your careers page, social media profiles, job postings, and all recruitment marketing materials should harmoniously echo the same message and visual identity. Use these platforms to highlight the real stars—your employees. Share testimonials, success stories, and the benefits of working at your organization. Show potential candidates the vibrant, supportive, and dynamic environment they'll be joining.

Remember, an authentic and consistent employer brand not only attracts talent aligned with your values but also excites them about the journey ahead. Craft your narrative with care, and let it speak volumes about who you are and what you represent.

Leveraging Technology in Recruitment

Technology has transformed the recruitment landscape, making it more efficient and effective than ever before. Tools like Applicant Tracking Systems (ATS), Artificial Intelligence (AI), and specialized recruitment software streamline many of the traditionally time-consuming tasks, such as resume screening, candidate communication, and interview scheduling. By leveraging these technologies, recruiters can focus their efforts instead on high-value activities, such as building meaningful relationships with candidates and assessing cultural fit (chemistry).

An ATS revolutionizes the recruitment process by managing everything from posting job ads to onboarding new hires. It centralizes candidate information, tracks application status, and facilitates seamless communication. AI-powered tools further enhance this process by analyzing resumes, matching candidates to job requirements, and even predicting candidate success based on historical data.

Video interviewing platforms have opened up new possibilities, enabling remote interviews that save time and resources. These platforms also expand the talent pool, allowing candidates to interview from anywhere in the world.

> *While technology brings efficiency, maintaining a human touch remains crucial.*

However, while technology brings efficiency, maintaining a human touch remains extremely crucial. Many candidates are now using AI to tailor their resumes to job ads and descriptions, which may not accurately reflect their true skills. Therefore, it's vital to stay engaged throughout the recruitment process, looking beyond polished resumes, being certain to identify candidates with genuine knowledge, experience, and passion.

Personalize your communication with candidates, provide timely feedback, and strive to create a positive candidate experience. Remember, technology should complement, not replace, the essential human elements of recruitment.

Create a Remarkable Candidate Experience

Establishing a remarkable candidate experience is crucial in attracting and retaining top talent. Candidates who enjoy a positive experience are more likely to accept job offers, recommend your organization to others, and remain engaged throughout the hiring process.

Effective communication is key to a positive candidate experience. Providing regular on-going updates on the status of their application (with transparency about timelines) and responding promptly to candidate inquiries goes a long way. Personalized communications to the candidate demonstrates genuine interest and appreciation for their time and effort. I have shared with my staff over the years that we have to keep the candidates warmly engaged. When we allow the lines of communication to grow cold, the "fish jump off the hook."

Respect candidates' time by streamlining the interview process. Minimize the number of interview rounds and ensure interviews are well-organized and efficient. Provide clear instructions and feedback at each stage of the process. For example, let them know who they're meeting with and the job titles for these individuals.

Cultivate a warm and inclusive atmosphere during interviews. Equip interviewers with the skills and training needed for effective conversations. Ensure candidates feel at ease and valued, providing ample opportunities for them to ask questions and delve into your organization. It's crucial to remember that an interview is a dialogue, not a monologue. Too often, hiring managers forget the importance of candidate questions, which can lead to a disconnected experience. A heartfelt, two-way conversation creates a powerful connection and significantly increases the likelihood of a candidate accepting an offer if it's the right fit.

The Advantage

Recruitment excellence is not just a process, but a strategic advantage that shapes the future of your organization. I've had the pleasure of participating in one of these most significant hires. Let me share it with you.

In the bustling city of Nashville, Tennessee, our mid-sized, global non-profit faced a critical challenge. Our Chief Financial Officer of 37 years decided to retire but the prior executive leadership team failed to institute a succession plan. As a highly trusted non-profit with a global reach, we needed to attract top-tier talent to meet our ambitious goals of reshaping the financial structure of the organization. However, the job market made it difficult to find the right people.

Recognizing the importance of strategic recruitment, our Chief Executive Officer, Craig Warner, allowed me to revamp our hiring process. We began by defining our employer brand while emphasizing our commitment to financial integrity and global impact. We wanted candidates to see our organization as not just a place to work, but as a place to grow, contribute, and make a difference for a higher purpose. We understood that the ideal candidate needed not only exceptional skills and experience but also a deep alignment with our faith and a shared passion for our mission to make a profound impact in the world.

After an exhaustive search and numerous candidate interviews, we decided to restart the entire hiring process. Even though we identified some strong candidates, something wasn't quite right.

I was recently a new hire myself, serving as the head of human resources. Within two weeks of the restart, I received an email about a candidate currently serving as Chief Financial Officer for one of the largest consumer packaged goods companies in the world. He had a tremendous track record, but his income level and future options were significantly higher than the non-profit compensation range for this position. Everyone discouraged me from pursuing this candidate, considering it a "waste of time." However, I felt compelled to explore this opportunity. He was a highly experienced Chief Financial Officer with a track record of global success.

During the interview process, he was not only compelled by our vision and global reach but also felt genuinely welcomed, needed, and called to the opportunity. The interviews were more like conversations, providing him with ample opportunity to ask questions and deeply understand our organization's culture and mission.

What made the difference was our commitment to fostering a heartfelt and emotional connection. We took the time to show this candidate the impact he could make, introduced him to the team, and even shared stories of past challenges he might encounter and help us correct. No stone was left unturned. We made it clear at the same time he wouldn't earn his accustomed compensation. However, this approach made him feel like he could truly make a global difference.

Ultimately, he accepted the offer, and his impact was immediate. His character, leadership, and expertise helped drive the organization to significantly higher levels of efficiency while also remaining under budget. More importantly, his alignment with our values and his dedication to the community inspired the entire team. His leadership and excellence became a cornerstone of our financial position and a beacon of our commitment to excellence and global impact.

This story highlights the power of a strategic and heartfelt recruitment process. By prioritizing character, calling, cultural fit (chemistry), and creating a welcoming environment, we attracted a candidate who was not only highly skilled, shared our vision and values, but even accepted a significantly reduced compensation package because of the calling. The right people can truly drive an organization forward, turn challenges into triumphs, and foster a culture of success and purpose.

I challenge you to embrace these principles in your recruiting efforts. Seek out individuals who not only possess the necessary skills but also resonate with your organization's mission and values. Create a predictive hiring process that reflects the heart and soul of your organization, ensuring candidates feel valued and inspired. Have some fun with it! Remember, finding the right people can transform your organization and make a lasting impact that extends far beyond the immediate role. Let's commit to hiring with intention, integrity, and a passion for making a difference.

Chapter 5

ASSESSMENT
More Than a Gut Feeling

"How we hire impacts who we hire."
—John Vlastelica

It was the best of hires; it was the worst of hires.
It was the age of insight, it was the age of impulse;
It was the era of data, it was the era of gut instinct.
It was the season of clarity; it was the season of confusion.

Chris Brown, the CEO of Lighthouse Consulting, stared across the conference table at the candidate. On paper, Emily Sandoval looked like the perfect fit: a solid education, a résumé packed with accomplishments, and glowing references from people whose names alone could open doors. Yet, something gnawed at Chris as he skimmed her application for the fifth time.

"She's got the credentials," he thought, drumming his fingers on the table. "But is she the right one for the team? I have been burned before."

He thought back to a specific hiring misstep a couple of years ago—a confident, smooth-talking manager who dazzled in interviews but fizzled under pressure. That hire cost the organization months of progress, and tens of thousands of dollars. Chris had sworn then to stop relying solely on gut feelings. But even now, despite having armed himself with personality tests, competency-based assessments, and structured interview questions, the doubt lingered.

"So, Emily," Chris began, leaning forward, "tell me about a time you faced a major setback at work and how you handled it."

Emily did not miss a beat. She launched into a well-rehearsed anecdote about leading a struggling project team, her tone confident, her delivery polished. But Chris caught something—a slight hesitation when he asked a follow-up question. Was she telling him what he wanted to hear or what really happened?

The challenge in modern hiring, Chris realized, is not just finding someone qualified; it involves peeling back the layers of practiced answers and polished personas to uncover the real person underneath. That is where assessments are effective. They are not checklists; they are mirrors, reflecting the true capabilities of a candidate in ways that even the sharpest intuition might miss. Assessments provide insights into the behaviors and psychology of employees. They give you insights into what you will receive from an employee once the interview is over and the 90-day acclimation is complete.

As Emily wrapped up her answer, Chris nodded thoughtfully. This was not about gut versus data; it was about how the two could work together. His instinct told him Emily had potential, but the assessments he had prepared would be the final judge. This time, he knew the hiring decision would be made on more than a gut feeling.

> *... our society has shifted towards prepackaged responses rather than genuine thoughts and real answers.*

Isn't this a familiar scenario? Candidates come well-rehearsed and armed with polished answers to your questions. During a business trip to Nigeria several years ago, I stumbled upon a book titled *Great Answers to Tough Interview Questions* by Martin John Yate. It is a best-selling guide for job seekers, providing scripted answers to common interview questions. While I appreciate the idea of helping candidates prepare, our society's shift from genuine thoughts and real answers to pre-packaged responses struck me deeply.

As candidates become more adept at professional interviewing, are you equally prepared to see through the polish and determine the heart of their true capabilities? This chapter on assessments and the next chapter on screening provide direction for adopting behavior-based interviewing and leveraging assessments. If you grow in your own skills with these various tools at hand, you can ensure that the real person—the genuine Emily Sandoval—is discovered. This approach will help you uncover the true essence of each candidate, beyond their rehearsed answers.

Transforming the Hiring Landscape

In recent years, the approach to screening and online pre-employment testing dramatically shifted. While initially the focus was streamlining the hiring process by cutting costs and reducing time-to-hire, today's leading employers prioritize more than just efficiency. They are seeking innovative solutions from their talent management teams to gain a competitive advantage. The goal has shifted towards creating a selection process that identifies well-prepared candidates who can drive business success.

Pre-employment assessments are now a crucial tool for employers, providing a standardized method to evaluate potential employees' skills, knowledge, personality traits, and cognitive abilities. These assessments allow organizations to make more informed hiring decisions by identifying candidates who best fit the job requirements and the organizational culture.

Top Pre-Employment Assessments

To objectively measure a candidate's abilities and potential fit, organizations now reach beyond mere resume information and interview impressions by utilizing these types of assessments:

- **Cognitive ability assessments:** Measures a candidate's general mental capability, including logical reasoning, numerical ability, and verbal comprehension. These help predict how well a candidate can think, learn, solve problems, and assimilate new information.
- **Technical skills assessments:** Evaluates a candidate's ability to perform specific job-related tasks. For example, these include coding tests for software developers or typing tests for administrative roles. They ensure that candidates have the necessary skills to perform the job.
- **Personality assessments:** Explores a candidate's behavioral traits and characteristics, such as extroversion, agreeableness, and emotional stability. These assessments help determine cultural fit projecting how a candidate might interact with other team members.
- **Integrity assessments:** Measures honesty, reliability, and ethical behavior.
- **Work sample assessments:** Provides candidates with tasks similar to those they would perform on the job to evaluate their practical skills.

Employing a combination of these assessments can provide a comprehensive understanding of a candidate's abilities, personality, and fit for the role, leading to more informed hiring decisions and better overall outcomes.

Hard Skills vs. Soft Skills

As we navigate the realm of assessments in The Predictive Hiring Model, imagine you are building a dream team for a championship game. You would not just choose players based solely on their physical prowess, would you? No, you would also consider their ability to work with the team, stay calm under pressure, and communicate effectively on the court or field.

In the same vein, when evaluating potential hires, focusing exclusively on hard skills—those quantifiable abilities like technical knowledge or specialized training—without considering the soft skills can be a game-losing strategy. Just as a team needs both physical strength and strategic collaboration, a successful organization thrives on the perfect blend of hard and soft skills.

Let us dive into why it's crucial to seek out candidates who excel in both arenas. We will explore how hard skills get the job done, while soft skills ensure it's done right, fostering an environment where innovation, teamwork, and resilience flourish.

Understanding Hard Skills

Think of hard skills as an athlete's ability to make a free throw, kick a field goal, or spike a volleyball. These are the technical skills honed over time with practice. While practice does not make perfect, it certainly increases the likelihood of success. Similarly, in the professional world, hard skills are the concrete abilities and knowledge that individuals develop through education, training, and experience on the job.

What Are Hard Skills?

Hard skills are specialized abilities that can be demonstrated through certifications, degrees, portfolios, or work experience. They are essential for effectively performing job-specific tasks and are often prerequisites for employment in various fields. Here are some examples to provide a clearer picture:

- **Technical Proficiency**: Proficiency in programming languages (e.g., Python, Java), using software (e.g., Microsoft Excel, Adobe Creative Suite), or IT knowledge.

- **Data Analysis**: The ability to interpret data, use statistical software, and perform quantitative research which drives decision-making.

- **Project Management**: Knowledge of project management software (e.g., Trello, Asana), methodologies (e.g., Agile, Scrum), and budgeting.

- **Foreign Languages**: Proficiency in speaking, reading, and writing in languages other than your native language, facilitating communication in global contexts.

- **Mechanical Engineering**: Skills in CAD software, blueprint reading, and machinery operation crucial for designing and manufacturing products.

How Do We Assess Hard Skills?

Assessing hard skills involves using a variety of tools and methods to accurately measure a candidate's technical abilities and knowledge. Here are some effective ways to evaluate hard skills:

- **Technical Assessments**: Assign coding challenges, technical problem-solving tasks, or software-specific tests. For instance, ask a programmer to write code or debug software.

- **Work Samples**: Review portfolios or work samples that highlight the candidate's previous projects, designs, or work-related products.
- **Certifications**: Verify relevant certifications and licenses that validate the candidate's expertise in a specific area, such as PMP for project management or CPA for accounting.
- **Skill Assessments**: Use standardized tests to measure proficiency in specific skills, like electrician skills assessment involving wiring diagrams and troubleshooting electrical systems or language proficiency exams for translators.
- **Simulations**: Conduct job simulations that mimic real job tasks, allowing candidates to demonstrate their skills in a controlled environment, like creating a mock project for a project manager to plan and execute.

Importance of Matching Hard Skills

Effective assessment is about comparing job applications against the already established hard skills criteria in our job descriptions. Ask, "Is there a preliminary match in job responsibilities, core competencies, education, and experience?" Matching the hard skills first is crucial because, as appealing as a great personality might be, it cannot compensate for a lack of essential abilities.

During my tenure as the head of HR for a custom software and IT Development company, I often encountered the need to verify an applicant's proficiency in various software applications. Based on the position, rigorous testing of these skills was essential to ensure competence. Tools like those from TestGorilla™ proved invaluable, offering detailed insights into candidates' abilities while helping to identify high-potential individuals. Such assessment instruments provide a comprehensive understanding of an applicant's capabilities, ensuring that only the most qualified and capable candidates are selected.

Understanding and accurately assessing hard skills is critical for making informed hiring decisions. While hard skills are crucial, they must be complemented by soft skills to ensure a well-rounded and capable team.

Understanding Soft Skills

Just as an athlete's technical skills must be complemented by strategic thinking and teamwork, professional success hinges on both hard and soft skills. Soft skills are personal attributes and interpersonal abilities that enable individuals to function in the workplace effectively.

I will never forget the time I learned the hard way about the importance of soft skills. Early in my career I worked for a tremendously gifted leader. Once she requested that I create a thorough "Ideal Candidate Profile" for a specific position within our business. Up to that point I had never even seen an "Ideal Candidate Profile" let alone written one. Additionally, the internet was not robust with examples, and I never thought to ask her more questions about the project.

Instead, I suffered in silence. I pulled an "all-nighter" at the office until 2:00 a.m. creating the document I believed she wanted. Exhausted, I emailed it to her at that early hour and finally went home. I was so eager to impress her that I just could not bring myself to ask her any questions and ultimately appear as if I didn't know what she needed. I dove in headfirst without any thought of collaborating or communicating with her or anyone on my team.

When I arrived back at the office later that morning, following a short nap, I encountered her wrath and frustration because I delivered a product that was completely opposite of what she needed. My boss was angry because not only had I not provided what she asked for, I also failed to ask for her clarification. Instead of reaching out for help, I isolated myself, convinced that I had to prove my worth by solving everything on my own.

She called me into her office and gently pointed out that while my technical skills were top-notch, I lacked the soft skills of communication, teamwork, and stress management. My boss recommended that I start over by asking questions about the project and the required deadline with her. I had wrongly assumed she needed it immediately, but she did not need it for another week.

Taking her advice to heart, I began to check in with her and ask the necessary questions. To my surprise, she was willing to outline the product she needed and provided me with other examples of "Ideal Candidate Profiles" that offered valuable insights. This made the project more efficient and even enjoyable. By leaning on each other's strengths, we developed a much-needed document, and I met the deadline. This experience taught me that no matter how skilled we are technically, it is our ability to connect, communicate, and collaborate with others that truly drives success.

Soft skills, much like an athlete's capacity to adjust to emotional variables in competitive sports, are crucial. This includes maintaining level-headedness under pressure, valuing teamwork over individual recognition, and respecting a coach's instructions. In the professional world, this translates to problem-solving, interpersonal communication, tactfulness, collaboration, and business writing.

What Are Soft Skills?

Soft skills are intangible abilities related to how individuals interact and approach their work.

Here are some examples:

- **Communication**: Conveying information clearly and effectively.
- **Teamwork**: Working well with others and fostering collaboration.

- **Problem-Solving**: Identifying issues and developing effective solutions.
- **Time Management**: Prioritizing tasks and managing deadlines.
- **Adaptability**: Being flexible and adjusting to new situations.
- **Leadership**: Inspiring and guiding a team toward goals.
- **Emotional Intelligence**: Managing emotions and recognizing others' emotions.
- **Conflict Resolution**: Navigating and resolving disagreements constructively.
- **Work Ethic**: Demonstrating reliability and dedication.
- **Followership:** Supporting and following the direction of leaders effectively, demonstrating engagement, and the ability to work well within the leadership structure.

How Do We Assess Soft Skills?

- **Behavioral Interviews**: Asking candidates to describe how they handled specific situations.
- **Situational Judgement Tests (SJT)**: Presenting hypothetical scenarios to assess responses.
- **Role-Playing Exercises**: Simulating real-life work scenarios to observe how they handle specific situations.
- **Personality Assessments:** Using tools like DISC to understand tendencies and fit.
- **Peer Feedback**: Gathering insights from colleagues and supervisors.

Importance of Soft Skills

Most often, underperformance isn't due to a lack of technical skills but to a deficiency in soft skills. In my experience, aside from layoffs, every employee's termination stemmed from issues with soft skills. Their relational and emotional quotient is low. While people acknowledge the importance of developing hard skills, soft skills are often overlooked. Early identification of these shortcomings can prevent hiring errors. Soft skills are crucial as they boost performance, retention, productivity, morale, and customer satisfaction, all while fortifying the leadership pipeline.

Understanding and assessing soft skills is crucial for building a high-performing team. Combining soft skills with hard skills creates a balanced, capable, and cohesive team. In my experience, technically driven companies are far more successful when all team members possess a blend of hard and soft skills. As I've interviewed throughout the years, incorporating many behavior-based questions and role-playing exercises ensures we hire well-rounded individuals who work within their strengths.

HARD SKILLS	SOFT SKILLS
The expertise necessary for someone to successfully do the job.	*The personal attributes you need to succeed in the workplace.*
Examples:	**Examples:**
• Technical Proficiency	• Communication
• Core Competencies	• Critical Thinking
• Education	• Leadership
• Experience	• Adaptability
• Specific Knowledge	• Teamwork
• Specific Abilities	• Conflict Management
• Speaking Foreign Languages	• Emotional Quotient
• Writing & Editing	• Problem Solving

Common Pitfalls

When it comes to using assessments in hiring, there are several common pitfalls to avoid.

The following is a list of these pitfalls to help you identify and avoid them.

Improper Training

The biggest challenge is often a lack of training about how to effectively deploy these tools. Without proper training, assessments can be easily misused, leading to poor hiring decisions and even negligence. The presence of an assessment doesn't automatically translate to better hiring outcomes. Everyone involved in the process needs to understand how to both administer the assessments and interpret the results within the broader context. This includes considering the candidate's potential boss, the dynamics of the team they will join, and the specific responsibilities of the position.

Ensuring that everyone is properly trained in the deployment and interpretation of assessments is vital. When used to their full potential, these tools lead to improved hiring decisions, better team integration, and greater overall success for the organization.

Lack of Alignment

As discussed earlier, alignment is a crucial factor. When I share about alignment with assessments, I mean ensuring that the candidate's attributes and capabilities fit well with the role, the team, and the organizational culture. For instance, if you hire a visionary young professional with high potential, it's vital to place him or her in an environment where his or her strengths can thrive, rather than pairing each with a manager who has an inflexible, by-the-book mentality.

Misalignment can lead to frustration, underperformance, and ultimately loss of the individual.

As an example, I recently consulted with a CEO where a highly visionary employee was managed by someone who demanded meticulous list-checking for maintenance tasks. This mismatch in expectations caused significant friction. By aligning duties with individual abilities and ensuring managers are aware of their team's dynamics, you can maximize effectiveness and job satisfaction.

Start at the Top

To implement or improve the use of assessments, start at the top. Ensure that the CEO and senior leadership are fully on board. Their buy-in is critical to overcoming skepticism and resistance within the organization. By establishing a solid foundation of support from the top, you can create a culture that values strategic assessment and integrates it effectively into the hiring process.

For example, I had an employee who was being disruptive and toxic, particularly concerning the assessment tool our organization used. This behavior sometimes stems from insecurity or perceiving the data as a threat. I had to address it directly, making it clear that while skepticism is fine, toxicity is unacceptable. The CEO decided on a specific direction for the organization, and it was imperative that every employee align with this vision or reconsider their place in the company. Without the CEO's backing, skeptics within the organization can become divisive, creating a negative undercurrent. In this situation, it was crucial to ensure everyone was on board and working towards the same goals to maintain a positive and productive work environment.

Alignment must be comprehensive, from top to bottom. The CEO's decision to use assessment tools to grow the company sustainably is a first step. Equipping everyone and embedding the tools into the process is the next. By aligning roles and duties according to individual abilities, and making sure managers understand their own situation, you can maximize everyone's potential.

Moreover, it is important to recognize that every trait or profile has its benefits and drawbacks. For instance, an assertive and independent individual who takes initiative can also come across as overly strong. This duality means that while someone may excel in certain areas, they might require support in others. Using data as a strategic tool, not a weapon or shield, helps in understanding and leveraging these traits effectively.

Assessment Fatigue

Another common pitfall is assessment fatigue, where organizations use so many different tools in the hiring process that they lose their effectiveness. Candidates may become weary of being constantly assessed, viewing them as just another trend rather than a strategic tool. To avoid this, it is crucial to find an assessment tool that your organization can become comfortable with and trust. Consistency and familiarity with a chosen tool can provide more reliable insights, especially when your team is excellent at administering and interpreting the results of the assessment.

Superman or Superwoman?

When every job description seems to demand a superman or superwoman candidate, it is essential to distill those expectations into realistic, attainable qualities that align with the role and the person's natural strengths. While you will never find the perfect person, you can still get a lot of what you want. By using a data-driven process, which leverages human analytics, you can design a position based on specific inputs and then write the job ad or descriptions from those inputs. Essentially, you write the ad based on the results of the inputs. Since the inputs themselves are initially in a vacuum; you do not fully understand what you're describing until the process is complete. This approach helps ensure the position aligns closely with your actual needs, leading to the right new hire for your organization.

Collaboration

Collaboration is key when filling an open position. It is essential to gather data from all relevant stakeholders—hiring managers, peers, supervisors, and next-level managers. However, many companies lack a comprehensive strategy for utilizing these tools effectively. Inst]ead of integrating them into their hiring processes, they often resort to using them in a superficial manner, such as during off-site retreats, only to shelve them afterward without a clear strategy.

This approach is arbitrary and fails to leverage the full potential of these tools in making informed hiring decisions.

Advantages of Pre-Employment Assessments

Assessment data can significantly improve hiring decisions and overall hiring quality. Some of the advantages of pre-employment assessments are:

- **Reduced hiring time:** Narrow down the candidate pool to those most qualified. This is where such tools can help you speed up the process.
- **Improved quality of hire:** Select candidates with the necessary skills and potential for success.
- **Increased fairness:** Standardized testing helps eliminate bias in the selection process.
- **Better cultural fit:** Identify candidates whose personality aligns with the organization's values.

During a recent consultation, one of my clients had a hiring experience that served as a valuable lesson in the importance of data-driven decision-making. They needed to hire a comptroller and ended up selecting a candidate who was, according to assessment data, the most social, friendly, non-detailed, and laid-back person imaginable. The interviewers were charmed by his personality and made their decision based on this initial impression.

However, this approach overlooked a critical factor: whether the candidate fit the necessary profile for the job they had developed. The result was a poor hiring decision because the selection was based on surface-level traits rather than The Five Attributes (explained in the chapter about screening) and capabilities that assessments could have revealed.

This experience underscores the risk of relying solely on personality during the hiring process. Instead, hiring decisions should be grounded in the insights provided by comprehensive assessments. These tools help identify candidates' true potential, ensuring they possess the skills and characteristics essential for success in the role. It is crucial to look beyond the polished exterior and base decisions on data that align with the job's requirements.

Emphasizing this approach can significantly enhance hiring outcomes, leading to better matches and long-term success for both the employee and the organization.

Consistent Application

To integrate assessments effectively, gaining alignment from the top is essential. Ensuring that the CEO and senior leadership are fully on board is crucial for overcoming skepticism within the organization. Consistent application and trust in the data are key. Organizations should determine what they are looking for based on the metrics provided by their tools, rather than evaluating candidates without prior information.

Fair and Unbiased

Ensuring that an assessment is fair and unbiased requires a high validity rating. High validity tools significantly reduce bias, making it crucial to follow the test design strictly to avoid creating biases during administration. There is also the issue of test-retest validity, where familiarity with the test can introduce bias. Well-designed assessments include safeguards to detect and mitigate such attempts.

Ultimately, using assessments effectively in the hiring process involves a strategic and comprehensive approach. By understanding and leveraging the data, organizations can make informed hiring decisions that go beyond superficial impressions, leading to better alignment and higher success rates.

Design in Using Assessments

In summary, key elements of using a well-designed assessment in the hiring process include buy-in from leadership, strategic objectives, and comprehensive application beyond hiring into management and retention. Another key element is to ensure every manager is equipped with the requisite knowledge to interpret and apply the data effectively. It is crucial to integrate these assessments into regular conversations about performance and team strategies, determining who fits where and what roles suit them best. If assessments are treated as just another HR tool, shelved after hiring, their impact is minimized.

Best Practice

In my experience, providing an established baseline understanding through a two-day workshop increases every positive benchmark for the organization. No one should gain access to the tool without this training. Otherwise, you introduce malpractice. Also, ongoing support through highly knowledgeable advisors is imperative. This ensures that your organization makes the most of its investment by leveraging expert advice whenever needed. Implement consulting rhythms that include regular calls and direct access to advisors via phone, making certain continuous support is implemented.

Despite rigorous efforts, some organizations still struggle with the effective use of assessment tools. For instance, it is not uncommon for business owners and senior leaders to struggle to believe in a tool's effectiveness. This skepticism, combined with some misaligned results, can contribute to challenges in its acceptance and application. Sometimes, data is ignored or undervalued, affecting retention and placement success. In other situations, a team may end up with all members demonstrating similar profiles, creating a lack of diversity in thought and approach. This scenario illustrates the risk of failing to cover organizational gaps, akin to a baseball team having no left-handed pitchers in the bullpen.

Alignment does not mean hiring the same type of person across a division. Diversity of thought and abilities are crucial, especially at the leadership level. Consistency in leadership styles can be effective, but it is essential to avoid creating "mini-me" teams where diversity of thought and approach is lacking.

Building Trust through Reliability

To use assessments effectively, it is vital to trust the data. The validity of assessment tools is paramount, with some achieving up to 90% accuracy, significantly increasing hiring success rates from the commonly cited 50-50 chance to the high 80s or low 90s. While the Equal Employment Opportunity Commission (EEOC) does not explicitly state a specific percentage for validity when it comes to hiring assessments, it does use the "four-fifths rule" (also known as the 80% rule) as a guideline to identify potential adverse impact.[10] This means if a protected group's selection rate is less than 80% of the group with the highest selection rate, it may trigger the need to demonstrate the validity of the hiring process. Even with high validity, it is crucial to understand that these tools are not crystal balls; understanding and leveraging the data is essential for informed hiring decisions. Reliability is also critical—consistency and reliance on these tools can make an enormous difference in hiring outcomes.

This continuous learning approach ensures you never settle, always seeking to refine and optimize the tool's application. Consider the nuances of each hiring situation, such as team dynamics, the leader's style, current strengths and limitations, and the long-term strategic vision for the role.

Regularly reviewing and improving your assessment tools and processes can significantly enhance hiring outcomes. By ensuring these elements are in place, your organizations can make data-driven, informed hiring decisions that contribute to your long-term success.

Case Studies

While I would like to share the names of various assessments I have utilized and that I recommend, my legal counsel has discouraged me from doing so. However, the following case studies involve companies that used some of my recommended tools with tremendously positive outcomes.

1. **Construction Industry Client**: This client was struggling with thinning margins and leadership false starts. By using an assessment tool and integrating it with senior management support, they identified the right qualities needed in an operations leader within their company. After placing the new leader in the role, the company saw increased profits and streamlined operations.

2. **Service Industry Client**: This client experienced continuous revenue and talent losses. By using hard and soft skill assessments for talent acquisition and management, they focused on putting the right people in the right seats. This led to a reduction in turnover from 80% to less than 6% and a 50% increase in revenue within two years.

3. **Aerospace Company**: An underperforming division within this aerospace company was losing money for over two years. The division leader utilized one specific assessment to identify hidden talent within the organization and restructured the team. Within 90 days, the division became cash-positive and started growing rapidly.

These real-world examples underscore the transformative impact of using assessments in hiring and talent management. By focusing on both hard and soft skills and employing the right tools, organizations can build robust, high-performing teams that drive business success and foster a cohesive workplace culture.

However, we must never remove the human and spiritual aspects of connecting with candidates. If we place the process on autopilot through instrument assessment and neglect the reality of God-created giftedness placed within each individual enabling each of us to discern hard skills versus soft skills, we have missed the aspect of humanity and the joy of developing our personal selection skills. Only God can give and cultivate the greatest gifts, which include discernment, wisdom, and insight. Relish these gifts. Make sure they are included in your predictive hiring process.

Chapter 6

SCREENING
Beyond the Resume

"The quality of your candidates is a direct reflection of the quality of your hiring process."
—John Vlastelica

Many of my family members possess a deep-rooted passion for college basketball. We often watch entire championship games standing, not sitting, in our living room. Standing... Shouting at the TV... Yelling at players as if we're in the stands and they can hear us... It's pretty amazing! It's just that exciting! Super fun!

In April of 2015, the head coach for the Kentucky Wildcats was John Calipari. He is undeniably one of the more prominent figures in college basketball and this 2015 team was the most important team as far as his legacy as a head coach. Whether you like Kentucky basketball or not, most could agree that Calipari is widely considered one of the top NCAA basketball coaches of all time. He has taken three different programs—UMass, Memphis, and Kentucky—to the Final Four, and he led Kentucky to a national championship in 2012. His impressive career record and ability to develop NBA-caliber talent cemented his legacy in college basketball history.

That year, the Kentucky Wildcats entered the NCAA Final Four with an impressive 38-0 record. They played the Wisconsin Badgers and were heavily favored to win because of their undefeated record and the overall talent of the team.

I recall watching a pre-game interview with Coach Calipari. The commentator asked him, "What have you been doing to prepare your team for this match-up with Wisconsin?" Coach Calipari's response was, "I just want them to play their game." The commentator pressed him further by asking, "Have you all watched game film of Wisconsin?" To which Calipari responded, "No."

I looked over at my family and predicted, "They're gonna lose this game." No one in our living room believed me. I was confident of it because I knew something they didn't know. Kentucky wasn't prepared. They didn't know their enemy. They didn't know the little things that made Wisconsin who they were. Keep in mind that Wisconsin also made it to the Final Four even though they were not undefeated.

Kentucky experienced a shocking defeat at the hands of the Wisconsin Badgers, who won 71-64. Analysts pointed out that one of the main reasons for Kentucky's loss was their lack of preparation—they never watched any game film on the Wisconsin team. They underestimated their opponent and thought they could simply rely on their own skills to win. This oversight cost them dearly. Being unprepared for Wisconsin's strategies and gameplay led to their first and only loss of the season.

The single most critical misstep hiring managers often make in this high-stakes game of hiring is—lack of preparation.

The single most critical misstep managers often make in this high-stakes game of hiring is—lack of preparation. This isn't just a minor oversight—it's a foundational flaw that can derail the entire hiring process. Without thorough preparation, hiring managers risk overlooking vital details, misjudging candidates' potential, and ultimately making costly decisions that not only cost them real dollars, but also real time and emotional energy.

To secure the best talent for your team, you must meticulously prepare for the candidates you interview, review their resumes, identify gaps, and formulate targeted behavior-based questions. This high level of preparation harnesses the transformative power of strategic screening, turning the tide in your favor.

> *"Candidates are evaluating the company just as much as the company is evaluating them. Therefore, we must be time sensitive. This demands preparation!"*
> — Steve Hayes

In conversations with recruiting giant Steve Hayes, he emphasized the importance of treating every candidate with the utmost respect. "Candidates are evaluating the company just as much as the company is evaluating them. Therefore, we must be time sensitive. This demands preparation!" If our process drags on and on, candidates will discern that we cannot make a decision, and they will lose interest.

Be proactive in making The Predictive Hiring Model process efficient, educational, and informative for both sides. It's not a one-way process. Approaching the process with humility, rather than arrogance, ensures we don't miss out on top talent. We must view candidates as current and future "customers" and treat them with the respect they deserve.

Ready for Actionable Steps?

Rather than dwelling on the pitfalls and missteps in candidate screening, which are many, I want to shift your focus to a proactive and effective approach. It's far more powerful to equip you with a model that enhances your ability to screen candidates successfully. This is your moment to transform your hiring process and harness the potential of strategic screening. Embrace The Predictive Hiring Model, and let's dive into the actionable steps that help you identify, evaluate, and select the best talent for your team. Ready to make a change? Let's go!

Behavior-Based Interviews and Listening Between the Lines

Early in my career, in one memorable interview, we tasked an experienced manager with hiring for a critical role. The candidate appeared promising on paper, but the interview quickly unraveled. The manager, unprepared and disorganized, fell back on cliché questions like, "Tell me about yourself" and "What's your greatest weakness?" Without follow-up questions or meaningful engagement, the conversation remained surface-level. The candidate's polished answers masked deeper issues and critical nuances were overlooked.

After the interview, the manager, feeling the pressure to fill the role, hired the candidate based solely on his resume and rehearsed responses. Within months, it became apparent that the new hire struggled with teamwork and failed to adapt to our organization's culture. This mistake not only led to missed project deadlines but also created a ripple effect of dissatisfaction among the team. The cost of a poor hiring decision was clear: increased turnover, lost productivity, and a demoralized team.

As a result of this experience, we realized our hiring process was fundamentally flawed. We began to uncover the various pitfalls contributing to the hiring mistakes including a lack of structure, inadequate preparation, and poor engagement. Determined to improve, we sought out new methods and discovered the transformative power of behavior-based interviewing which involves "listening between the lines."

The Fourth Discipline of The Predictive Hiring Model: Screening

The fourth discipline of The Predictive Hiring Model is screening. Screening employs multiple rounds of rigorous, systematic, behavior-based interviews with standardized competency-based questions while listening between the lines for specific responses. We also found post-interview debriefs to be very effective in evaluating and comparing candidates.

Transformative Practices

To overcome the shortcomings of typical poor interviews, behavior-based interviewing, and the art of listening between the lines are crucial. Instead of relying on generic questions, behavior-based interviewing focuses on specific past experiences and actions, providing a clearer picture of how candidates handled various situations. This technique involves asking questions like, "Can you describe a time when you overcame a significant challenge at work?" or "Describe an experience where you contributed to a team project under tight deadlines?"

Such questions not only reveal the candidate's competencies but also their problem-solving abilities, teamwork skills, and adaptability. By delving into real-life examples, interviewers can assess how candidates think, behave, and perform under pressure, offering a more accurate prediction of their future performance.

Listen Between the Lines & Listen More than You Talk

Moreover, listening between the lines is equally crucial. This involves paying close attention to the candidate's tone, body language, and subtleties in their responses. For instance, hesitation when discussing teamwork might suggest a lack of experience or difficulty in collaborative environments. Conversely, enthusiasm and detailed accounts of past successes can indicate a high level of engagement and competency.

To get the screening process right, you need an interview plan with targeted, behavior-based interview questions, such as the ones provided later in this chapter, as well as in *The Essentials of Hiring: The Five Attributes* book (featuring over 140+ behavior-based interview questions). These open-ended questions encourage detailed responses, and taking thorough notes helps you remember each candidate's specific answers. Seeking contradictory evidence by asking similar questions in different ways verifies consistency in their responses.

Allow for moments of silence during the interview to give candidates the space to think and respond more deeply. Prioritize listening over talking and engage candidates by asking follow-up questions about their responses. This approach encourages genuine answers and helps reveal true insights, as many candidates may attempt to manipulate responses to common questions. By probing further, you prompt them to think critically and authentically.

Choose Your Type of Interview

There are several types of candidate interviews that organizations can utilize to assess potential employees. Each type serves a different purpose and can provide unique insights into a candidate's suitability for a role. Some of the most common types of candidate interviews are listed on the next page.

By selecting a combination of these interview types, you can significantly enhance your hiring process. The initial phone interview acts as a gateway to gauge basic qualifications and allows for an unbiased approach to interviewing because you're primarily focused on comparing the candidate to the qualifications your job requires. Following this with the in-depth in-person interview assesses body language and interpersonal skills. Each interview type serves a distinct purpose. Video

> ## TYPES OF CANDIDATE INTERVIEWS
>
> 1. **Phone Interviews:** Initial screening to discuss basic qualifications & fit.
> 2. **Video Interviews:** Remote face-to-face interaction, assessing communication skills.
> 3. **In-Person Interviews:** Provides a deeper connection and assessment of body language and interpersonal skills.
> 4. **Panel Interviews:** Involves multiple interviewers, offering diverse and comprehensive perspectives.
> 5. **Group Interviews:** Multiple candidates interviewed together, assessing teamwork, communication, and competitive skills.
> 6. **Behavioral Interviews:** Focuses on past behavior and experiences to predict future performance.
> 7. **Technical Interviews:** Evaluates specific technical skills and problem-solving abilities.
> 8. **Case Interviews:** Presents real-life scenarios for candidates to analyze and solve, showcasing their analytical and strategic thinking.
> 9. **Stress Interviews:** Intentionally creates stressful situations to see how candidates handle pressure.
> 10. **Competency-Based Interviews:** Assess specific competencies or skills related to the job.
> 11. **Structured Interviews:** Follows a set list of questions to ensure consistency and fairness.
> 12. **Unstructured Interviews:** More conversational, allowing for a free-flow discussion and deeper insight.

interviews are indispensable because they offer a remote yet personal touch, allowing you to evaluate a candidate's communication skills and professionalism from a distance. This is vital when time and expense are factors.

By thoughtfully integrating the varied interview formats, you can paint a comprehensive picture of each candidate's potential, ensuring you not only fill the role but also enhance your team's synergy and performance. This multifaceted approach to interviewing transforms the hiring process, enabling you to make more informed, effective decisions and secure the best talent in the competitive job market.

Let's focus on a few more advantages.

Unleash the Power of a High Hiring Batting Average (HBA)

If there ever was someone who possessed a "Hiring Divinity," it was Karen Graham. Her abilities seemed almost otherworldly due to her remarkable "x-ray vision" for identifying the perfect candidates or seeing through them. In the realm of talent acquisition, Hiring Batting Average (HBA) is a critical measure of a manager's effectiveness in selecting candidates who not only fit the role but also thrive within the organization's culture. Individuals with a high HBA consistently make successful hiring decisions, resulting in engaged, productive, and loyal employees.

Karen exemplified this within our organization. As our most senior leader in Cost Accounting, her staff was fully engaged, demonstrating remarkable loyalty and enthusiasm for their work. They highly regarded her leadership and remained with the company for years. Recognizing her exceptional abilities, we requested that she join our select interview panel for leadership roles. Karen's outstanding HBA made her an invaluable asset to our interviewing team. Her unique ability to see through candidates allowed her to provide insightful feedback for crucial roles such as Plant Manager, R&D, IT, and Sales & Marketing positions.

Discovering and leveraging individuals with a high HBA on your interview panel leads to better hiring outcomes and stronger, more effective teams. These individuals bring a keen eye for talent, ensuring that selected candidates are not only qualified but also aligned with the organization's values and culture. This intuitive ability to discern potential and fit can revolutionize the hiring process, significantly reducing turnover and fostering a motivated, cohesive team.

Collaborative Interviewing

In addition to having interviewers with a high HBA, involve multiple stakeholders with a focus on alignment. Define clear roles for each interviewer—one person might focus on assessing chemistry (cultural fit), while another evaluates competence (technical skills), and another looks at problem-solving abilities. As part of The Predictive Hiring Model, we create a consistent evaluation criterion that everyone uses to assess candidates, so the team can compare "apples to apples." This framework integrates both hard and soft skills, as well as alignment to team values, while including diverse perspectives that ensure a balanced view of each candidate and reduces unconscious bias.

The Five Attributes

As an established formula, many have come to appreciate that The Five Attributes or "the 5 C's" of hiring are character, calling, chemistry, competence, and contribution.

While each of these is defined and expressed at length in my sister book, *Essentials of Hiring: The Five Attributes*, allow me to share briefly about each, as they are nested within the screening discipline of The Predictive Hiring Model.

The Five Attributes of Hiring

	Components related to SOFT SKILLS	Components related to HARD SKILLS
Character	✓	
Calling	✓	
Chemistry	✓	
Competence	✓	✓
Contribution	✓	✓

Character

In virtually every workshop I've held in the past 10 years, it's inevitable that someone will ask, "Is there priority on these 5 C's? To which I reply, "Yes." Character is always a first priority, as someone cannot give what they do not possess, and I cannot help someone improve their character.

Character is often revealed through consistent actions, decisions, and behavior, especially when challenging circumstances arise. It's about doing the right thing even when no one is watching and maintaining integrity regardless of the circumstances. In essence, character defines who we are at our core and how we respond to the world.

I recommend you ask candidates how they're feeding and developing their character. Ideally, the right candidates will cite examples of reading great books that demonstrate a balanced life of personal devotion or that reveal their values.

Here are a few questions we sometimes ask related to this attribute:

- Can you describe a time when it was necessary to make a difficult ethical decision at work? What was the situation and how did you handle it?

- Tell me about a time when you faced a conflict with a colleague. How did you resolve the situation?

- What is the hardest thing you have needed to forgive in the workplace? How did you handle it? Are you still dealing with it?

So, what are some practical examples of how you fireproof your hiring and evaluate your candidate for character? Allow me to share a story from Dr. Mark Rutland's book, *Hanging By A Thread* (see next page).

STORY FROM *HANGING BY A THREAD*

J.B. Wise had been the president of his organization for four decades. He wondered how many bright-eyed young executives he had interviewed and hired in those years. He liked people, especially young people he could take under his wing and mold them into profitable producers.

He had to admit that these two applicants were good. Very good! In fact, it grieved him not to hire them both, but he only had one opening. As the waiter cleared away the dishes, he analyzed the eager young hopefuls across from him.

Young Bill Goodman was a tech graduate. He was knowledgeable, soft-spoken, and slightly bookish.

Jim Quisling, on the other hand, was an Ivy League graduate, and even though he was slightly unsure on a few of the more technical points, J.B. Wise definitely leaned in the direction of Quisling.

"Do you mind if I ask a question now?" Bill Goodman asked. "My wife advised me to get a clear reading on one point, and I really trust her counsel."

J.B totally ignored Goodman's question. Instead, he seized the moment to test Quisling. "What about you Jim? Did your wife send you off with any questions in hand?" Stated with condescension in his tone.

"Hardly," Quisling snickered. "She wouldn't know what to ask."

J.B. Wise chuckled and leaned close, hoping to draw Quisling on. "No head for business, eh?" "No head for much of anything, actually," Quisling answered. "A classic beauty from Boston."

The two men shared the joke.

"And your wife?" J.B. spun around to face Bill Goodman, hoping to rattle him. "Does she always tell you what to ask?" "She certainly doesn't control me if that's what you mean. But Alice is very bright, and I trust her advice in many areas of life. She's really a wonderful person. I wish you could get to know her."

In that one moment J.B. Wise knew he had his man. Quisling, the Ivy League puffin, had mocked his own wife during an interview. What would he say about the company in an unguarded moment?

J.B. Wise looked forward to meeting Bill Goodman's wife.[11]

Calling

Calling is a sense of vocation, especially one believed to be divinely inspired. Within this attribute, we seek to understand if individuals are self-aware. Do they know their calling?

Surprisingly, through the fulfillment of literally thousands of interviews, I've learned most candidates don't possess a solid sense of their gifts or calling. Nor do they know what to do with their gifts if they are aware. Even with all the self-help books in the marketplace, there's a tremendous deficit of self-awareness and even self-discovery that ultimately leads to this awareness of one's gifts.

We hope to determine if a candidate is seeking work as "just a job" or is it the fulfillment of their gifts?

Here are a few questions we sometimes ask related to this attribute:

- Tell me about a moment in your career when you felt you were truly making a difference. What was the situation, and how did it impact your perspective on your work?
- Unfortunately, only a small percentage of people know what they really love to do and who they are. What is it that you love to do and how did you discover "This is me!"? How did you come to understand this calling?
- Can you share a specific example of a project or task that made you feel deeply fulfilled or particularly passionate? What did you enjoy most about it?

Chemistry

One of the most significant lessons I've learned in my career is that cultural fit is paramount. Skills and experience are important, but they can be developed over time. Cultural fit, on the other hand, is intrinsic. Chemistry is the alignment of values, beliefs, and behaviors between the individual and the organization. When there's a strong cultural fit, employees are more engaged, motivated, and committed to the organization's success.

Consider The Ritz-Carlton, renowned for its world-class service and luxury accommodations. The company's success is rooted in its strong culture, which emphasizes unwavering commitment to customer service, excellence, and teamwork. The Ritz-Carlton's motto, "We are Ladies and Gentlemen serving Ladies and Gentlemen," encapsulates the values and behaviors expected from every employee.

The Ritz-Carlton's hiring process is meticulous and focused on finding individuals who embody their core values. During the hiring process, candidates undergo multiple interviews that assess not only their skills and experience but also their alignment with the company's service-oriented culture. Behavioral interview questions such as, "Can you describe a time when you went above and beyond for a customer?" help identify candidates who naturally strive for excellence and demonstrate a passion for service.

Here are a few more questions you may want to ask related to this attribute:

- Can you describe a time when you had to collaborate with a group of people to complete a project? How did you make certain everyone's contributions were valued?
- Tell me about a time when you felt particularly connected to a team or organization. What factors contributed to that sense of belonging?
- Describe an instance where you navigated a challenging interpersonal situation at work. How did you handle it, and what was the outcome?

Competence

In the context of hiring, competence is the knowledge, skills, and abilities a person possesses, enabling them to effectively perform specific tasks and responsibilities required by a role. It might be technical expertise in hard skills (e.g., tools, systems, processes) and soft skills (e.g., communication, problem-solving, adaptability) necessary to meet or exceed the expectations of the position.

Competence is typically measured through resumes, interviews, skills assessments, and reference checks. While crucial, it's equally important to consider this quality alongside other attributes like emotional intelligence, chemistry, and trustworthiness.

Many employers place a heavy emphasis on competence. While it's undeniably important for achieving high performance, it's not always the most valuable attribute—except in highly specialized roles (such as a surgeon or air traffic controller). Balancing competence with other factors ensures a well-rounded and effective team.

Here are a few questions you may want to ask about this trait:

- If your manager gave you nine assignments to complete in one week and you genuinely felt you could only accomplish five of them, how would you handle the situation?
- Can you describe a time when you were forced to solve a particularly challenging problem at work? How did you approach it and what was the outcome?
- Tell me about a time when you were expected to learn a new skill quickly to complete a project. How did you manage it, and what did you learn?
- Describe an instance where your expertise made a significant impact on a project or team. What was the situation and how did your contribution make a difference?

Contribution

Contribution is what a candidate brings to an existing team or project immediately and in the long term. Peter Drucker highlights that contributions should include results-oriented thinking, alignment with organizational goals, a focus on strengths, and collaboration.

When candidates embody character, calling, chemistry, and competence, this contribution attribute flows naturally.

When I'm evaluating candidates for this attribute, I know these are individuals who go the "Second Mile." They are "Multipliers" as described by Liz Wiseman in her book *Multipliers*. They amplify the capabilities of those around them and foster an environment where everyone thrives and exceeds expectations. Such candidates not only contribute their own skills but also elevate the entire team's performance, driving sustained success and innovation. When candidates embody character, calling, chemistry, and competence, this attribute of contribution will flow naturally.

To make certain you have high HBA (Hiring Batting Average) interviewers, it's crucial to prioritize finding the right people. If these interviewers are not available within your organization, seek them externally. I became close friends with a small business owner of a communications firm in Franklin, TN, early in both of our careers. He invited me into his business to interview every senior team member he hired over a ten-year period. It was a joy to watch his business grow and see each new leader make significant contributions to the company's culture. This growth was driven by their adherence to these attributes and their value-based approach to running their business. Today, his business has grown more than tenfold.

Here are four questions to ask about this attribute:

- It will help me to know you better if you tell me what you think are your best skills?
- Can you describe a project or task where you took the initiative to go above and beyond your typical responsibilities? What motivated you and what was the outcome?
- Tell me about a time when you had to work collaboratively with others to achieve a significant goal. How did you contribute to the team's success?

- Describe a situation where you identified an area for improvement within your work or team. What actions did you take to address it and what were the results?

Candidate Interview Plan

If you're looking for a well-structured interview plan, this can help you select the right candidate. Follow these steps to make your process thorough, objective, and effective. However, don't forget that many types of interviews are available to you during the course of the hiring process. Use these steps as needed:

- Plan a logical, structured interview that includes pre-planned interview questions.
- Recognize the importance of developing an interview plan based on a thorough knowledge of the job to be filled.
- Understand that a behavioral example is a specific life-history event—used to determine the presence or absence of a skill.
- Probe further and seek out behavioral predictors.
- Use interviewing techniques that allow for interviewer control, such as silence.
- Make selection decisions based on facts and information—not on gut feeling.
- Use the concept of "the best predictor of future behavior is past behavior" and how it is important in the behavioral-based interview process.
- Understand why some questions cannot be legally asked in the interview process.

By following this plan, you'll create a structured, compliant, and evidence-based approach to interviews, ensuring your decisions are grounded in fact and aligned with the role's requirements.

Post Interview Debrief

To ensure you achieve the utmost excellence in the screening process, conduct a thorough post-interview debrief. Having led these vital meetings for years, I can attest they can be a tremendous capstone of the hiring journey. It is very exciting when stakeholders gather to share invaluable feedback about candidates.

I always invite every interviewer to these debriefs. If I've asked someone to take the time to interview a candidate, it's essential to seek their input. Neglecting this step often leads to visible disappointment and confusion among interviewers.

Here are some very practical steps to help you:

Set a Structured Debrief Meeting

- **Set a Time & Agenda in Advance:** When scheduling all interview times, include the debrief meeting on the calendar and invite all interviewers as well as the hiring manager.
- **Involve All Interviewers:** Be sure all interviewers participate in the debrief to provide a comprehensive perspective and make certain they cover all key points. The debrief may have to be modeled several times until it begins to feel more natural.
- **Feedback Before Meeting:** Invite interviewers to submit their feedback independently before the debrief to prevent groupthink. This has worked very well for me over the years.

Objective Evaluation

- **Use a Scorecard:** Create and use a standardized scorecard for assessing candidates on key criteria. I recommend The Five Attributes Scorecard found in the Predictive Hiring Toolkit at www.PredictiveHiringModel.com.

- **Take Notes:** Take notes during each interviewer's feedback and retain those recommendations to review later.
- **Focus on Specifics:** Discuss specific examples of a candidate's responses rather than general impressions.

Open Communication

- **Encourage Candid, Insightful Feedback:** Foster an environment where interviewers feel comfortable sharing their true opinions. Challenge vague statements like, "They weren't a good fit" by asking, "What did they say or do that leads you to think that?"
- **Discuss Strengths and Weaknesses:** Thoroughly assess the candidate's strengths and areas for improvement.

Consistency and Fairness

- **Compare Against Criteria, Not Each Other:** Evaluate candidates based on predefined criteria rather than comparing them to each other.
- **Check for Bias:** Be vigilant about potential biases and address them during the discussion.

Conclusion and Next Steps

- **Summarize Key Points:** End the debrief with a summary of the discussion and a consensus on the candidate.
- **Decide on Follow-Ups:** Determine any follow-up actions or additional steps needed before making a final decision.
- **Give Interviewers Opportunity to Support or Oppose the New Hire.**

By incorporating these practices, your post-interview debriefs will be more productive and help you make fantastic hiring decisions.

Reference Checks: Most Overlooked Goldmine of Insight

I can already hear the skepticism: *"Reference checks are useless." "No one says anything worthwhile anymore." "Why bother?"*

I respectfully disagree. In my experience, reference checks consistently reveal deeper insights into a candidate that were not previously available. The issue isn't whether reference checks work; it's the perspective you bring into the process.

Here are the top three reasons organizations skip reference checks:

1. **Time Constraints & Lack of Process**: Reference checks are time-consuming, and most organizations lack a standardized process for conducting them. As a result, they prioritize speed over reference insights.

2. **Privacy Concerns**: Concerns about violating privacy laws or regulations may deter companies from performing reference checks. This shouldn't deter you from gathering the appropriate information.

3. **Overconfidence**: Hiring managers feel confident in their gut-feeling judgment and rely on their assessment rather than external references who have already worked with the candidate.

Reference checks are more than a formality, they're a key step in making informed hiring decisions. Here's why:

1. **Verify Information:** Ensure the candidate's resume is accurate by confirming employment history, job titles, and achievements.

2. **Gauge Performance:** Former supervisors and colleagues provide insights into work ethics, reliability, and strengths, offering a clearer picture of the candidate's abilities.

3. **Assess Cultural Fit:** Learn how the candidate worked within teams, adapted to workplace culture, and managed interpersonal relationships.

4. **Understand Work Behaviors:** Discover how the candidate manages stress, conflict, and feedback, helping predict their behavior in your organization.

5. **Identify Red Flags:** Spot potential risks like negative patterns or ethical concerns that might not surface during interviews.

6. **Confirm Skills & Competencies:** Validate both hard and soft skills, ensuring the candidate is truly qualified for the role.

7. **Mitigate Risk:** Protect your organization from negligent hiring claims by showing you performed due diligence.

Incorporating reference checks into your hiring process provides invaluable insights, helping you make more informed decisions. When you ask the right questions of current or former employers, you're almost guaranteed to uncover information that deepens your understanding of the candidate. See our reference check guide to assist you in the process.

To get the most value from each reference call you make, consider using this opening statement: *"When I spoke with John [Candidate's Name], he assured me you'd be open to sharing your insights about him—his strengths, his work, and even areas where he could grow and develop. This conversation is ultimately for his benefit and growth."*

How Many References Should You Check?

There's no magic number of calls to make. The goal is to gather feedback that confirms the candidate meets or exceeds your position's requirements based on The Five Attributes. However,

I recommend you only perform reference checks on your #1 and #2 candidates after the screening discipline. By limiting it to your top two candidates, you can focus on really digging deep to understand your top finalist rather than performing shallow reference checks on many.

The objective is simple: Trust but verify. Every reference call should bring clarity and insight you owe to your top two finalists.

Planning for Hiring Success

I want to underscore a fundamental truth that resonates deeply within the realms of hiring: "If you fail to plan (and prepare), you are planning (and preparing) to fail." Benjamin Franklin's axiom holds especially true in the hiring process. Thorough preparation and meticulous planning are not just steps in a procedure. They are the very foundation of securing the right talent. Without a clear plan, our efforts can lead to missed opportunities, inefficiencies, and ultimately, failure to attract the best candidates. In practice, this means we craft a seamless candidate experience.

International Case Study from Dida Fava, São Paulo, Brazil

I close this chapter with an international case study from Dida Fava, São Paulo, Brazil (see next page).

INTERNATIONAL CASE STUDY — Dida Fava, São Paulo, Brazil

The wisdom of Solomon has been proven over the centuries to be credible. In Proverbs 26:10, he communicates, "Like an archer who wounds at random is one who hires a fool or any passer-by." This wisdom resonated deeply with Dida Fava when she first encountered the concept of "The 5 C's of Hiring." This framework proved to be transformative in her hospital healthcare setting.

"I learned from Chad Carter's Essentials of Hiring: The Five Attributes that character is the foundation upon which all other attributes are built. This truth became evident as I was managing an innovation department in a Latin American healthcare organization, facing the challenge of building a new team. One particular situation highlighted the importance of prioritizing character alongside competence.

"A highly skilled employee, despite their technical prowess, began displaying isolating behaviors and resistance to teamwork. As Carter astutely observes, 'We hire on skills. We fire on behavior.' This resonated with our experience, reminding us that technical excellence without character and collaborative spirit can be detrimental to an organization's health.

"Guided by the 5C's principles—Character, Calling, Chemistry, Competence, and Contribution—we approached the situation with wisdom... prioritizing character in the workplace. The resolution came naturally as we focused on acknowledging the employee's technical contributions while being honest about the misalignment with our values of collaboration and character integrity. Carter notes that when character and competence align, extraordinary results follow. The employee's departure, though necessary, was handled with dignity and respect, setting a precedent for the entire team.

"This experience transformed our hiring approach. As Carter emphasizes, 'Calling provides the 'why' behind the work.' We began prioritizing character, calling, and chemistry in our recruitment process, understanding that competencies could be developed once these foundational attributes were present.

"The results were remarkable. Within two years, the department grew from 8 to 30 employees, maintaining an impressive 93% retention rate. Most remarkably, the department's vibrant culture earned its distinction as the organization's best workplace environment - a testament to the power of values-based leadership, particularly noteworthy for an innovation hub not primarily focused on financial metrics.

"The impact of this approach is further validated by exceptional employee engagement metrics. Currently, the department boasts an extraordinary Employee Net Promoter Score (eNPS) of 83—a figure that places it firmly in the "best-in-class" category. To put this achievement in perspective, while Bain & Company considers scores between +10 to +30 as "good" and +50 as "excellent," our score of +83 represents a level of employee advocacy that far exceeds industry benchmarks.[12] This metric, which measures employees' likelihood to recommend their leaders and company to others, powerfully demonstrates how prioritizing character and calling alongside competence creates not just a productive workplace, but one where people truly thrive.

"Carter's insight that contribution flows naturally when character, calling, competence, and chemistry are present proved true in our experience."[13]

This testimony stands as a witness to the practical application of this wisdom in modern healthcare management. As Proverbs guides us in selecting workers with discretion rather than hastily hiring based on skills alone, we found that integrating principles with professional practices led to sustainable success and a flourishing workplace culture.

Chapter 7

OFFERING
How to Seal the Deal

"Pay attention to the details."
—CHAD CARTER

The Dream Offer

We were working diligently to hire a highly sought-after data scientist, Lincoln, who was being courted by several companies. Lincoln expressed interest in the position. However, he was noncommittal during the interview process, mentioning concerns about the team culture and how the position aligned with his long-term goals.

After the final interview, Stephanie decided to go above and beyond making a standard offer. Instead of making a quick phone call, Stephanie invited Lincoln for an informal coffee chat to discuss next steps. During this meeting, Stephanie did something unexpected: she presented a customized "Welcome Package," which included a personalized offer letter detailing how Lincoln's work could directly impact our company's mission, specific projects Lincoln would lead, and a roadmap of how the role aligned with his career aspirations. Stephanie was an excellent listener throughout the hiring process.

To address Lincoln's concerns about team culture, Stephanie gathered video messages from team members, each welcoming him and expressing excitement about their potential contributions. The videos included anecdotes about how the company fostered growth, collaboration, and personal development.

At the end of the meeting, we presented the formal offer letter in a sleek folder with a handwritten note on the cover that said, *"Lincoln, we believe in you, and we're excited to build the future together."*

Surprised and moved, Lincoln confessed that he was leaning toward another company but was now reconsidering. Stephanie, sensing the moment, asked directly, "What would it take for this to feel like the perfect next step for you?" He candidly shared a few final thoughts about flexibility and relocation assistance, which we committed to address immediately.

The next morning, Lincoln called Stephanie and said, "The thought and care you put into this offer showed me that this is the place I belong. I'm in!"

This true story illustrates how personalization, empathy, and a strategic approach can convert a simple offer into an irresistible opportunity. Would you like to create dream offers like this?

The Fifth Discipline is Offering

Great organizations aren't just defined by what they do, but how they do it. The way they present an offer leaves a lasting impression on candidates. These organizations excel in the art of making offers, understanding that every step of the hiring process—listening, discerning, and pre-closing—builds to this pivotal moment. Any organization, regardless of size, can achieve this! If you can dream it... You can do it.

When we prioritize building an emotional connection during the recruitment discipline, a genuine and warm-hearted response naturally follows. It's a testament to the trust and rapport built throughout the process, creating a strong foundation for successful professional relationships. Nurturing this connection not only enhances the candidate's experience but also reinforces the organization's values and culture.

This is what I've aimed to cultivate in every team I've led. Just like an orchard yielding fruit, it produces wonderful results. And I delight in seeing a flourishing outcome that makes dreams come true for both the new hire and the team.

What's Important To You?

Many years ago, I learned a powerful question from a real estate friend. This single question dramatically improved my hiring results. I experienced the common scenario where we invested a great deal of time and energy into a candidate only to have the candidate decline our offer. I sensed that we were missing something. In conversations with my real estate friend, he brought up the concept of a "pre-closing conversation" with his clients and that almost 100% of the time he would close the sale because of this simple question that unearthed his client's root issues. It is so simple that most overlook it. He would ask the client, "What's important to you?" This simple query can unlock the key to successful hiring.

Let me share a story that illustrates this perfectly. We were in the process of hiring a Plant Manager for our largest manufacturing facility. The President of the company already offered the candidate an impressive package—a generous sign-on bonus, a car, an inflated relocation package, and a fully paid Executive MBA program. Yet, the candidate still remained hesitant to accept.

The President called a small meeting with our CFO, COO, VP of HR, and myself—the Director of Human Resources at the time. After twenty-five minutes of brainstorming with no viable solutions, I raised my hand. "Yes, Carter?" the President asked. I asked, "Would you like me to land the plane?" He asked, "Can you do that?" I confidently said, "I believe I can." "How long do you need?" he inquired. "48 hours," I responded. "Done," he agreed.

I immediately left the meeting and called the candidate. After genuinely checking in with him, I asked, "Jim, if I removed all of the various components that we've discussed with you previously and we made you a new and fresh offer, can you tell me what's important to you in that offer?"

He replied, "The education of my children."

The plant was located in a rural area with poor public schools. I asked if he knew of any schools in the area he might be interested in his children attending. He mentioned a specific school and its cost. I proposed structuring a package to cover this, and then asked, "If we made you an offer that encompassed this vitally important area for you and your family, would it make a difference and could we expect that you would come and join our team?"

He responded enthusiastically, "It sure would make a difference. And my wife would be happy!"

I returned to our President and provided him with the good news. He was astonished at how quickly this had been resolved—especially after weeks of discussions.

Key Takeaways

1. **Ask the Right Questions**: Understanding what's truly important to the candidate can make all the difference.
2. **Listen Carefully**: Sometimes, all it takes is listening to their needs to craft an offer that speaks to their heart, mind, and needs.

3. **Tailor the Offer**: Customize the package based on their priorities, not just standard cookie-cutter perks that you think everyone desires.

This experience taught me the importance of personalizing job offers and truly listening to the candidates' needs. It's a practice I've carried with me ever since.

Crafting the Perfect Job Offer: A Personal Approach

Job offers have so many variables. As a result, I'm not going to attempt to give you every scenario. However, I want to provide you with some important nuances. Crafting a fantastic job offer involves more than just presenting an attractive compensation package.

Nuances of the Job Offer:

1. **Personalization**: Tailor the offer to the candidate's specific needs and preferences, which you can gauge from previous conversations. This shows that you listened and care about what matters most to them. Make them feel desired, valued, excited, and confident about joining your organization.

2. **Total Rewards**: Highlight the full range of benefits, not just the compensation. Include information about health benefits, retirement plans, bonus potential, professional development opportunities, and paid time off (PTO) work-life balance benefits.

3. **Clear Communication**: Be clear and concise in your offer letter. Break down each component of the offer and explain it in simple terms. Avoid jargon that might confuse the candidate. Be consistent with your job description. If the responsibilities shift during the candidate's journey with you, it doesn't produce confidence in their experience with your organization.

4. **Excitement and Enthusiasm**: Convey genuine enthusiasm about the candidate joining the team. A positive and welcoming tone can make a significant impact.

5. **Flexibility**: Offer flexibility where possible. To some candidates, flexible hours are vitally important, as are remote work options, or tailored benefits. This can make the offer more appealing.

6. **Future Growth and Opportunities**: If your organization is sincerely diligent in developing your staff, then emphasize the opportunities for growth. Highlight the potential for career advancement, skill development, and other long-term benefits. However, do not make commitments you're not willing to support.

7. **Support and Integration**: Assure the candidate that they will receive the necessary support and resources to succeed in their role. Mention onboarding programs, mentorship opportunities, and team integration plans.

8. **Timing and Follow-Up**: Be mindful of timing. Present the offer promptly and follow up to address any questions or concerns the candidate might have. This shows respect for their decision-making process. The offers I make include a timeframe. While the candidate can share with me their immediate acceptance, I offer them a five to seven-day conditional offer. You don't want an open-ended timeframe.

9. **Cultural Fit**: Reinforce how the candidate's values and goals align with your organization's culture. This helps the candidate envision themselves thriving within the organization.

10. **Transparency**: Be transparent about the offer's components and the decision-making process. This builds trust and credibility with the candidate.

By incorporating these nuances, you can create a compelling job offer that not only attracts top talent at all levels of your organization but also cultivates an emotional connection, compelling them to join your team.

Before extending the job offer, I meticulously detail the offer in writing. Having already had the "What's Important to You?" conversation with the candidate, I understand their priorities if they've been transparent.

This preparation allows me to use the written job offer letter as a comprehensive reference when I call the candidate. Since I've already had the "What's Important to You?" call, they're anticipating my offer.

I typically start the conversation with…"John, allow me to get right to it. We want to make you an offer. We want you to join our team because we believe you will enhance our story and we believe we can enhance your story, too. It's a win-win."

Total Rewards

So often, companies make numeric job offers and lose candidates because it's solely based on the salary number and what the benefits are. This is so wrong. It's a terrible path to travel.

Instead, create a "Total Rewards" path.

Let me share a story to illustrate this. I was hiring an administrative assistant who was going to work directly for me. When it came down to the numbers, I knew we would have a lower salary number but a much higher benefits number than any place else where she might interview. So, I asked her if the salary number was healthy enough for her to accept the role? She replied with great certainty, "No."

In light of her response, I asked if she wouldn't mind dropping by our offices for a final visit. I knew I needed to show her the offer on a whiteboard and to walk her through the details.

I drew a T chart (see illustration on next page) and wrote all of the items on the left that her current employer offered.

I placed a dollar value next to every item.

Next, we compared her current situation with our offer, presenting it in clear, black and white terms. The decision became easy for her. She recognized the exceptional company culture we offered—something that can't be quantified and which her current employer couldn't match. As Peter Drucker famously said, "Culture eats strategy for breakfast!"

Remember that rational drivers, such as compensation, should remain in their category. Otherwise, when not explained properly they transition to emotional drivers and when people are driven by emotion, they often make illogical decisions. Compensation and benefits become emotional when less than skilled individuals have this discussion and clarity doesn't exist. But it's so easy to fix this by using the total rewards statement on a whiteboard to help communicate this. It simplifies everything. The comparison made it clear that our total rewards were superior. We watched the light bulb come on in her eyes.

CURRENT EMPLOYER		FUTURE EMPLOYER	
Compensation: $24/hour	$49,920.00	Compensation: $23/hour	$47,840.00
Retirement: 3% Match	$ 1,497.60	Retirement: 8% Contribution	$ 3,827.20
Vacation: 15 days	$ 2,880.00	Vacation: 15 days	$ 2,760.00
Holidays: 9 days	$ 1,728.00	Holidays: 12 days	$ 2,208.00
Medical: (Annual Co. Contribution)	$ 8,660.00	Medical: (Annual Co. Contribution)	$12,830.00
TOTAL	$64,685.60	TOTAL	$69,465.20

Key Takeaways:

1. **Rational vs. Emotional Drivers**: Keep compensation discussions rational to avoid them becoming emotional. Clarity in communication is essential.

2. **Total Rewards Statement**: Use a visual aid like a whiteboard to simplify and clarify the offer, making it easier for the candidate to see the full value.

By taking this personalized and transparent approach, you not only make the candidate feel valued but also ensure they fully understand the benefits of joining your team.

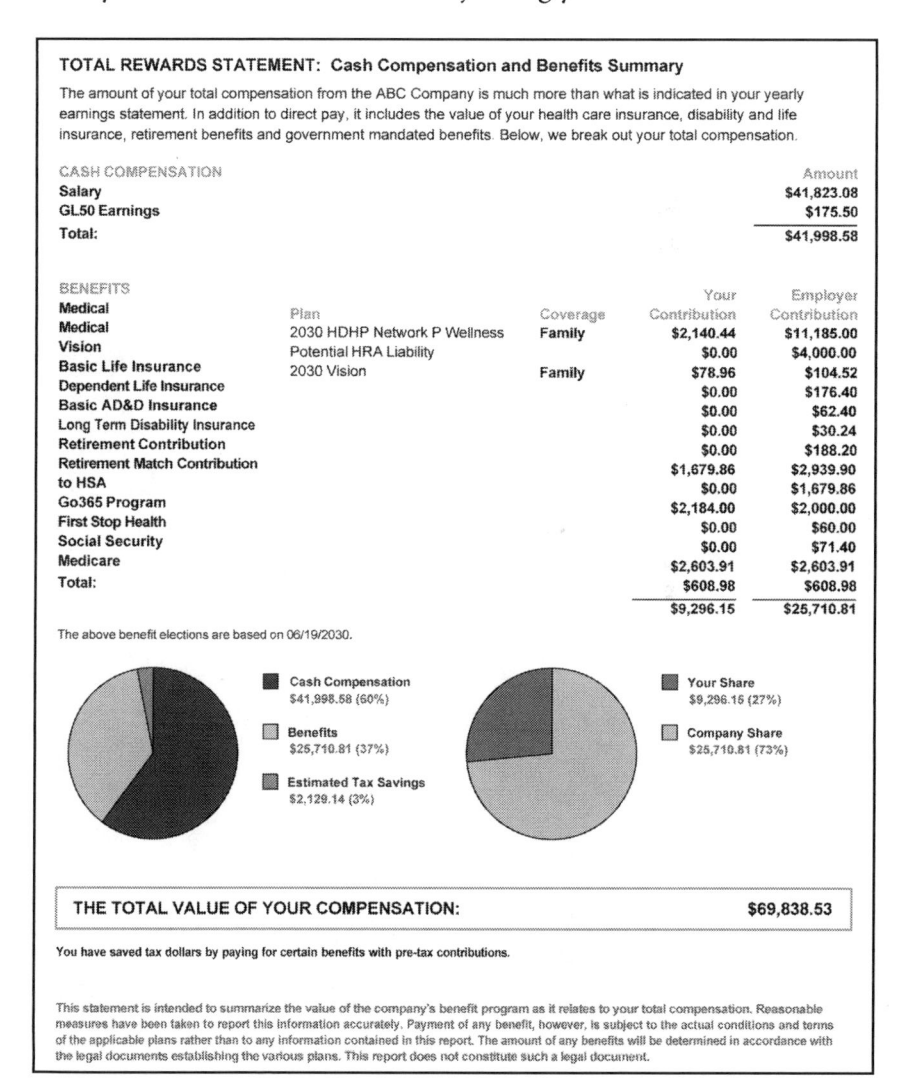

TOTAL REWARDS STATEMENT: Cash Compensation and Benefits Summary

The amount of your total compensation from the ABC Company is much more than what is indicated in your yearly earnings statement. In addition to direct pay, it includes the value of your health care insurance, disability and life insurance, retirement benefits and government mandated benefits. Below, we break out your total compensation.

CASH COMPENSATION				Amount
Salary				$41,823.08
GL50 Earnings				$175.50
Total:				$41,998.58

BENEFITS	Plan	Coverage	Your Contribution	Employer Contribution
Medical				
Medical	2030 HDHP Network P Wellness	Family	$2,140.44	$11,185.00
Vision	Potential HRA Liability		$0.00	$4,000.00
Basic Life Insurance	2030 Vision	Family	$78.96	$104.52
Dependent Life Insurance			$0.00	$176.40
Basic AD&D Insurance			$0.00	$62.40
Long Term Disability Insurance			$0.00	$30.24
Retirement Contribution			$0.00	$188.20
Retirement Match Contribution			$1,679.86	$2,939.90
to HSA			$0.00	$1,679.86
Go365 Program			$2,184.00	$2,000.00
First Stop Health			$0.00	$60.00
Social Security			$0.00	$71.40
Medicare			$2,603.91	$2,603.91
Total:			$608.98	$608.98
			$9,296.15	$25,710.81

The above benefit elections are based on 06/19/2030.

- Cash Compensation $41,998.58 (60%)
- Benefits $25,710.81 (37%)
- Estimated Tax Savings $2,129.14 (3%)

- Your Share $9,296.15 (27%)
- Company Share $25,710.81 (73%)

THE TOTAL VALUE OF YOUR COMPENSATION:	**$69,838.53**

You have saved tax dollars by paying for certain benefits with pre-tax contributions.

This statement is intended to summarize the value of the company's benefit program as it relates to your total compensation. Reasonable measures have been taken to report this information accurately. Payment of any benefit, however, is subject to the actual conditions and terms of the applicable plans rather than to any information contained in this report. The amount of any benefits will be determined in accordance with the legal documents establishing the various plans. This report does not constitute such a legal document.

Why We Always Have An Offer Letter: Building Trust from the Start

When I joined a fairly large organization, they had never experienced an HR function that genuinely partnered with the senior team to address staff needs. Instead, HR had traditionally taken an adversarial approach, focusing on enforcing policies and procedures rather than creating meaningful partnerships that solved problems and empowered employees. This shift towards collaboration was crucial in transforming the organization's culture and effectively supporting its people.

Within the first four to six weeks, I performed a gap analysis in which I discovered inconsistencies in how job offers were handled—some employees received verbal and written offers before starting while others didn't receive a written offer at all. This was an easy fix. I created several offer letter templates that reflected our shared values and provided the necessary details for all employees. My guiding principle for offer letters was clear: "If it's not in the offer letter, you don't get it." This meant that any expectations beyond the standard benefits, like more than the usual two weeks of vacation, needed to be discussed and agreed upon before the new hire's start date and it needed to be included in the written offer letter.

This new protocol was put to the test within weeks of implementation.

While I attended a conference out of state with our company president, our Manager of Talent Acquisition called me, clearly nervous. "I have one of our senior directors and a new employee questioning her paid time off. What should I do?" she asked. I responded, "Have you been using the job offer letter templates I provided and do you have a copy signed by both her and the hiring manager?" After a moment of silence, she said, "Give me a minute." When she returned, I could hear a smile on her face and relief in her voice.

The offer letter had pre-emptively resolved a long-standing issue. By implementing this simple protocol, we immediately addressed the confusion and eliminated the negative energy surrounding these discussions. She went up to the senior director's office with a copy of the offer letter, which had both his signature and the new hire's. We never heard about this issue from them again. This approach not only calmed our leadership and employees but also established a clear, consistent process that could have been implemented years earlier. It reinforced one of our guiding principles: to avoid misunderstandings by detailing all aspects of the offer and eliminating unnecessary noise within our organization.

Speak Your Values

The right people will naturally be drawn to your values, which will become shared values throughout your organization. This alignment should seamlessly extend into your job offers. Here's a robust example you might find useful, with various sections that can be customized or removed based on the needs of each new hire.

Ensuring your offer letter reflects your core values not only reinforces your organization's culture but also sets the tone for a strong, collaborative relationship right from the start.

To conclude Discipline #5: Offering, allow me to assist you in the process of writing offer letters with two examples on the next pages. I hope they are helpful to you!

OFFER LETTER — Example 1

January 1, 20xx

Ms. Jane Doe
123 Elm Street
Nashville, TN 37214

Dear Jane,

Welcome to ABC Company!

I am very pleased to confirm our offer to you for the {hourly non-exempt, regular, full-time} position of _____ – _____ Division in our Nashville, TN offices reporting to me.

At ABC Company, we are a values-driven organization. At the heart of our values is trust and respect for the individual. One way we demonstrate that trust and respect is by cultivating a compelling work environment where all associates can achieve their full potential. With that in mind, we are hopeful you will find this position to be a significant step toward a successful and rewarding opportunity that aligns with your vocational calling in life.

We have confirmed a start date of Monday, January 4, 2030, at 8:00 a.m. (CT). On that day, we will schedule a new hire onboarding process in our Nashville, TN offices to cover all of the necessary documents for payroll and benefit purposes.

Compensation and Benefits

Our offer to you is for an hourly rate of $__.__ which is $__,___.__ annually. Our payroll is bi-weekly and is paid through direct deposit. You will be eligible to participate in certain Benefit Plans during your first year of employment (i.e., Our Health Insurance is available on the first day of the month following thirty (30) days regular full-time service, as well as holidays, and a Healthcare Flexible Spending Account).

Additional benefits include life insurance, short and long-term disability, and a retirement planning option. These benefits are available after one (1) year of service. Information regarding our Benefit Plans will be discussed during your onboarding process.

Employment Eligibility

You may be aware that all U.S. employers are required by law to verify the identity and employment authorization for everyone hired. Therefore, on your first day of employment, please bring documents that verify your identity and authorization to work in the U.S. Acceptable documents include passport or driver's license and original social security card. An I-9 form, which details all acceptable documents, will be given to you during your orientation.

This offer and subsequent employment is contingent upon:
1. Verification of information supplied
2. Background Check
3. The understanding that you have no prior commitment with previous employers, such as restrictive agreements that would prevent you from fulfilling all requirements of your employment with ABC Company.

If this offer is acceptable to you, please sign and return a copy of this letter within the next seven days. Any employment resulting from this offer is employment-at-all. This simply means that both you and the company have the right to terminate the employment relationship at any time and for any reason.

Jane, please let me know if you have any questions or if there is anything I can do to help in getting you settled into your new position with us. I extend a warm welcome to you. We are looking forward to working together!

Sincerely,

Peter Drucker
Peter Drucker, Senior Director
ABC Company

cc: Personnel File

ACKNOWLEDGED AND ACCEPTED: *I have carefully considered this offer and believe it to be the right decision for me to serve at ABC Company.*

_____   _____
Jane Doe   Date

THIS IS NOT AN EMPLOYMENT CONTRACT

OFFER LETTER — Example 2

January 1, 20xx

Mr. John Doe
1234 Broadway
Nashville, TN 00001

Dear John:

On behalf of ABC Company, we are pleased to offer you an opportunity to respond to your calling for full-time service as our Data Scientist. Our entire Leadership Team is very impressed with you, your credentials, and your dedication. We believe that your contributions to our team will challenge us and move us to the next phase of growth, in alignment with our vision and purpose.

The terms of your new position with us are:

1. **Position.** Your title will be Data Scientist. You will be working out of our Home Office location in Nashville, Tennessee. You will report directly to me, and you will be responsible for all aspects of data accuracy and data driven solutions. This offer of employment is contingent upon ABC Company receiving satisfactory employment and background references on you which are well underway. In addition, we will require verification that you have no restrictive agreements that would prevent you from fulfilling all requirements of your employment with ABC Company.

2. **Start Date.** Subject to fulfillment of any conditions imposed by this letter, you will commence this new position as soon as you are released by your current employer. We anticipate your start date to be Monday, January 2, 2030.

3. **Proof of Right to Work.** For purposes of federal immigration law, you will be required to provide us with documentary evidence of your identity and eligibility for employment in the U.S. Please bring such documentation on your first day of employment.

4. **Compensation.**

    a. Base Compensation. Our offer to you is for an annual salary of $000,000.00 or $0,000.00 per bi-weekly pay period, subject to applicable tax withholdings and the organization's standard bi-weekly payroll schedule.

b. <u>Sign-On Bonus Compensation.</u> You will be eligible to receive a sign-on bonus of $00,000.00 upon the completion of the first payroll period when you commence your responsibilities.

In the event you voluntarily leave ABC Company prior to completing one year of employment, you will be required to repay the full amount of the sign-on bonus. In the event you voluntarily leave ABC Company after one year but prior to two years of service, you will be required to repay a prorated amount equal to 1/12 of the total for every month in which you are no longer employed.

5. **Benefits.**
   a. <u>Insurance Benefits.</u> Your cash compensation is supplemented by a comprehensive benefits program. You will be eligible to participate in our Benefit Plans currently available to other leadership team members on the first day of the month following thirty (30) days of regular full-time employment. Additional benefits include life insurance, employee assistance program, and flexible spending accounts.
   b. <u>Retirement Savings.</u> You are also eligible to participate in a retirement savings plan following one (1) year of service. ABC Company offers you a generous 6% contribution into a qualified savings plan with the ability to direct the investment of your contributions. Details of the plan will be provided to you under separate cover.
   c. <u>Paid Time Off.</u> You will be eligible for three (3) weeks of vacation time, plus six (6) personal days and nine (9) holidays in accordance with the organization's policies, as may be amended from time to time.

6. **Relocation.** ABC Company will provide you with a comprehensive relocation package to assist you with your move to Nashville. This package will include temporary housing, travel back and forth to Nashville, actual out of pocket moving expenses, closing costs for the sale of your current residence, assistance with closing costs if you should purchase a home and expenses related to house hunting for you and your family. You will work with relocation services on all of your relocation issues.

In the event you voluntarily leave the organization prior to completing one year of employment, you will be required to repay the full amount of all relocation expenses paid to you and to third parties on your behalf. In the event you voluntarily leave the organization after one year but prior to two years of service, you will be required to repay a prorated amount equal to 1/12 of the total for every month in which you are no longer employed.

continued

This letter sets forth the terms and conditions of your employment with ABC Company and supersedes any prior representations, whether written or oral.

This offer and subsequent employment are contingent upon:

1. Verification of information supplied
2. Drug Screen
3. Criminal Background Check
4. The understanding that you have no prior commitment with previous employers, such as restrictive agreements that would prevent you from fulfilling all requirements of your employment with ABC Company.

This employment offer is extended to you for seven (7) days from the date of this letter. If this offer is acceptable to you, please sign and return the enclosed copy of this letter to my attention. John, I am delighted to extend you this offer and look forward to having you on our team.

Sincerely,

Charles Dickens

Charles Dickens, *Senior Director*
ABC Company

cc: Personnel File

ACCEPTED AND AGREED:

_____
John Doe

_____
Date

THIS IS NOT AN EMPLOYMENT CONTRACT

Chapter 8

MEASURED OUTCOMES
Quantifying Success in Our Selection

"What gets measured gets improved."
—Peter Drucker

In many of our business decisions, and even in our life decisions, we rarely look back as we plan to move forward. It's important to consider past experiences and events so we can reflect and decide if we made wise choices. Taking a reflective posture on our decisions is a powerful way to gain insights and make better choices in the future ensuring greater predictability. After all, within the context of our organizations isn't this what we're being paid to do?

Of course, we're being paid to achieve fantastic results. But if we never reflect on the decisions we've made, we simply do the same thing, over and over again are achieving the same outcome, while expecting different results. Attributed to Albert

Einstein, this is said to be the definition of insanity. If we discipline ourselves to reflect and measure our outcomes, we gain a life practice that leads to greater confidence, less biased choices, and significantly better results.

Franklin, Tennessee captured my heart as a home for 30+ years. It's an easy community to love. It is quaint and filled with creatives in every arena of the arts, business, non-profits, and the church. One of my best friends, Stephanie, who is also deeply engaged in the HR leadership community, picked up on The Predictive Hiring Model a number of years ago. We loved to spar over different aspects of the model. I'm not sure if she realizes how much she actually helped me tweak the model and improve it.

Stephanie worked for a tech company. Constantly frustrated with the hiring decisions being made, she would share with me that it felt like whiplash. Because of The Predictive Hiring Model, she knew a better way, but since everything rises and falls on leadership, the president of the company just wanted her to hire candidates based solely on their impressive resume and technical skills. After many months of continual turnover, it became abundantly clear that these new hires struggled to collaborate with the team and often clashed with other colleagues. Stephanie, my friend, the HR Director, realized that she had overlooked The Five Attributes for the candidates during the hiring process.

Determined to learn from this experience, the HR Director and several of the hiring managers decided to implement a more holistic approach. They incorporated The Predictive Hiring Model and started including behavior-based interviews, team-based assessments, and reference checks that focused on soft skills and cultural fit. Over time, this new approach led them to hire candidates who not only had the necessary technical skills but also fit well with the team and company culture.

The Art of Reflection

This reflection and adjustment in the hiring process resulted in a more cohesive and productive team, demonstrating the value of learning from past mistakes and continuously improving hiring practices.

Research shows that the habit of reflection provides the ability to separate extraordinary professionals from mediocre ones. Again and again, we hear that making the time to reflect is a key to making yourself indispensable, not just today but into the future. Moreover, as far as we know, even artificial intelligence technologies can't perform this soft skill well.

Reflection is all about learning and looking back to measure the outcomes of previously made decisions. Did these decisions bring remarkable results or consequences? As you conduct an honest assessment of what worked and what didn't, you can decide what to do differently and how to move forward. Reflection requires courage because it is a thoughtful, deliberate, and. comprehensive process of transforming experience into meaning enabling you to shape the future. As described in a Fast Company article, it's a whole-body experience. "Being at the 'top of your game' only comes when you extract from your past how to engage the future."[14] Reflection in our hiring means looking at our processes and outcomes to determine what adjustments we need to make to improve. By doing so, we can make informed decisions that lead to better hiring outcomes, fostering a healthier and more productive workplace environment.

In the case of Stephanie, my HR colleague at the tech company, she analyzed exit interviews and conducted follow-up conversations with departing employees. Stephanie discovered that many new hires felt they weren't appropriately integrated into the company culture, leading to dissatisfaction and eventual departure. Armed with this insight, she revamped the onboarding process to include more cultural immersion activities and the integration of mentors.

Within six months, my friend saw a significant improvement in retention rates. By reflecting on her past decisions and making informed adjustments, Stephanie transformed her hiring outcomes and contributed to a more cohesive and satisfied workforce.

Key Metrics to Measure Success in Our Selection

To enhance the health of our hiring process, it's essential to identify, define, and measure several key metrics. These metrics serve as key indicators of our success or as areas where improvement is needed. Here are some critical metrics:

- **Retention Rates.** Retention rates offer a snapshot of how well new hires fit and stay within your organization. High retention rates indicate successful hiring decisions, effective onboarding processes, and effectiveness in how you assist the new hire in adjusting to the company culture. Conversely, low retention rates suggest a need for improvement in any of these three areas.

- **Time-to-Productivity.** This metric measures how quickly new employees become valuable contributors to your organization. When can the new hire actually perform independently what they were hired to do? This measure of productivity reflects the efficiency of our training programs and the clarity in which we developed our job roles (ideal candidate profiles). Faster time-to-productivity indicates that new hires receive the support they need to succeed quickly. When done successfully, we call this "fast tracking along the learning curve."

- **Quality of Hire.** Quality of hire evaluates the overall contribution of new hires, including their impact on productivity, revenue, and team dynamics. This metric can be assessed through performance reviews (30 days and up to 1 year), feedback from peers and supervisors, and the achievement of specific goals that were established before the individual even started into the role. High-quality hires will always positively influence the organization's bottom line and organizational health.

- **Quality of Sources.** Quality of sources measures the effectiveness and reliability of the channels and methods we used to attract our candidates. Were the channels and methods effective? Did we realize a high yield in the results of our recruitment strategies? Were job boards, websites, employee referrals, recruitment agencies, social media, career pages, job fairs, and college recruiting effective?

  If you assess the quality of your sources, you will realize where to focus your recruitment dollars and time and you will optimize your hiring strategies to achieve the greatest results. Your new hires will be examples of why you should either sustain your approach or refine it.

- **The Impact of Reflective Practices.** Reflective practices in hiring not only help in making better decisions but also foster a culture of continuous improvement. As stated earlier, encouraging hiring managers to reflect on their decisions and outcomes can lead to much higher levels of confidence in hiring, reduced bias, and better outcomes.

- **The Role of Feedback in Continuous Improvement.** Over the years, the HR teams I've led have consistently agreed on the importance of soliciting feedback from our candidates and new hires to drive continuous improvement. This practice has provided us with valuable insights that enhance each step of our hiring model and increase predictability. We achieved this through conducting surveys, follow-up interviews, and platforms like Glassdoor, which offer direct feedback from candidates to employers.

However, it's crucial to remember the principle: if you ask for feedback, you must act on it. Ignoring feedback is not an option.

Taking stock in the hiring process is a vitally important way to quantify success and make better decisions. By reflecting on your decisions, measuring key metrics, and making data-driven adjustments, you can transform your hiring practices and achieve greater organizational success. Remember, reflection is not just about looking back, it's about using the past to shape a more promising future.

Through The Predictive Hiring Model, we can create a systematic, repeatable process that delivers consistent, high-quality results. By embracing the art of reflection and committing to continuous improvement, we ensure that our hiring decisions lead to a thriving, dynamic organization where we truly enjoy the people we work with and love the work we do.

Chapter 9

THE CHALLENGE
What Action Will You Take?

"The best way to predict the future is to create it."
—Peter Drucker

Lastly, I want to underscore a fundamental truth that resonates deeply within the realms of hiring and selection: If we fail to plan and prepare, we are planning and preparing to fail. This axiom holds especially true in the hiring process. Thorough preparation and meticulous planning are not just steps in a procedure but instead are the very foundation for securing the right talent. Without a clear plan, our efforts can lead to missed opportunities and inefficiencies. Ultimately, not operating with an effective plan can lead to a failure to attract the best candidates who could create a stronger, cohesive team for our organization.

In practice, this means crafting detailed job descriptions, preparing insightful interview questions, and ensuring a seamless candidate experience. It means engaging all stakeholders, fostering open communication, and consistently reviewing and refining the recruitment strategy. By committing to this level of preparation, we not only enhance our chances of success but also build a reputation as an organization that values excellence and professionalism. This, in turn, attracts top talent who recognize and appreciate our intentionality in all we do.

Challenge: Build the Team Your Organization Deserves

You now have the tools to predict success in hiring. But tools and techniques are only as powerful as your commitment to use them. Hiring isn't just about filling seats—it's about shaping the future of your organization.

I challenge you to:

- **Define Your Standard.** Don't settle for "good enough." Be crystal clear about the values, skills, and mindset that define a great hire for your team.

- **Hold Yourself Accountable.** The Predictive Hiring Model requires discipline. Trust the process, even when it's inconvenient or tempting to rush ahead just to hire someone.

- **Invest in People.** Remember, the best hires don't just meet your expectations—they challenge them. Once you've brought the right people in, invest in their growth to unlock their full potential.

- **Measure and Reflect.** Hiring is a craft that improves with practice. Track your results, learn from your missteps, and refine your approach.

Great organizations aren't built by chance; they're built by leaders who are relentless about hiring the right people. Be that leader. Commit to this work not just as a strategy, but as a calling.

Peter Drucker is right. The choice is yours: Will you actively shape your future, or passively drift and hope for improvement? The power to create a better future for your organization lies in your hands.

ENDNOTES

1. Walter Frick, "What Research Tells Us About Making Accurate Predictions," *Harvard Business Review*, February 2, 2015.

2. Bob Buford, *Drucker & Me*, (Brentwood, Tennessee: Worthy Publishing, 2014), 166.

3. Peter Drucker, "Peter Drucker on Making Decisions," *Harvard Business Review*, June 21, 2004.

4. Patrick Lencioni, *The Five Dysfunctions of a Team: A Leadership Fable*, (San Francisco, California: Jossey-Bass, 2002).

5. Jim Collins, *Good to Great*, (New York, New York: HarperCollins Publishers, 2001), 41-42.

6. "Friedrich Wilhelm von Steuben," Wikipedia, last modified November 4, 2024, Friedrich Wilhelm von Steuben - Wikipedia.

7. American Naval Officer, Oliver Hazard Perry, 1813, Statement after defeating and capturing British Royal Navy ships in the Battle of Lake Erie.

8. Robert Henderson, Henderson's Line-Up, Grants Pass, OR, C12 Interview on YouTube, https://www.youtube.com/watch?v=lA-jSaRS3ci4&feature=youtu.be.

9. Dr. Tony Evans, *U-Turns,* (Nashville, Tennessee: B&H Publishing Group, 2020) 11-12.

10. Nathan Thompson PhD, "Four-Fifths Rule: Fair Employment Selection." *Assessment Systems*. December 8, 2023. https://www.assess.com/four-fifths-rule.

11. Mark Rutland, *Hanging By A Thread*, (Lake Mary, Florida: Creation House, 1991), 45-47.

12. Academy to Innovate HR (AIHR). (2024). Employee Net Promoter Score (eNPS): A Complete Guide. Retrieved from AIHR Digital.

13. Chad Carter, *The Five Attributes: Essentials of Hiring*. Franklin, Tennessee, Amazon, 2014.

14. James R. Bailey and Scheherazade, "Don't Underestimate The Power of Self-Reflection", *Harvard Business Review*, March 4, 2022.

ACKNOWLEDGMENTS

While this book is about "The Predictive Hiring Model," prediction is impossible without the rare quality of discipline. Without discipline, it is impossible to effectively achieve our desired outcomes.

Without discipline, predictions lack the necessary structure and consistency to be reliable. It's like trying to build a house without a foundation—no matter how good the design or materials, it will eventually crumble. Discipline ensures that data is collected methodically, analyzed rigorously, and applied consistently. This not only enhances the accuracy of predictions but also helps us understand the underlying patterns and trends that drive outcomes. In short, discipline transforms random guesses into informed forecasts. It allows us to simplify our processes—our way of doing things. The disciplines tell us where the boundaries lie.

I can't think of anyone who embodies and has demonstrated the aspects of discipline for me more than my father, Charlie Carter, mother, Wilma Carter, and two of my mentors, Jon Chew and Dewayne Thompson. Without their unique influences in my life, I certainly would not have pressed myself to discover more about my own strengths, gifts, and limitations.

I want to take this opportunity to tell you a little more about each not only to acknowledge them but also to express my deepest appreciation for their contributions in my life.

Charlie & Wilma Carter — I had a front row seat, 24/7, with one of the most disciplined and loving couples on earth. They are the ideal example of how to live a disciplined life. They seemed to automatically wake up every morning at 5:00 a.m. and immediately started their day. Even now during their retirement years, they still get up early and quickly complete their daily work. They are well known for excellence in everything they put their hands to accomplish. We live in a time when few people even understand the meaning of hard work. My parents demonstrated focused hard work and discipline every day through being a man and woman of character and competence. They were intentional about cultivating healthy soil within the foundation of my life. They taught me by example. They never asked anything of me they weren't willing to do themselves. As an example, I would be remiss if I failed to mention they always made space for God, others, and the things that really matter in life. They made an indelible and positive contribution in my life. Thank you, Mom and Dad, for the life lesson of discipline and your consistent focus on a relationship with God while caring for the needs and concerns of others being most important as well.

Jon Chew — I was incredibly blessed to attend The Baylor School in Chattanooga, Tennessee, from seventh grade through my senior year of high school. While there I experienced many influences, but none compares to the personal and tangible influence of my friend, teacher, and cross-country coach, the late Jon F. Chew. He affectionately referred to each one of us cross-country runners as "The Chosen Few of Chew." Under his direction, we won an unprecedented 110 dual meets in a row. Hardly a day passes that I don't think of him because of his great courage, discipline, and tenacity. He lived 18 of his 40 years with a rare form of melanoma cancer. Following each of more than 100 surgeries with sutures still fresh, he would somehow celebrate each one with a same-day run of six or so miles, possibly a bike ride, or a tennis match. Regardless of his personal situation he was determined to remain upbeat and demonstrate to us how "to go the extra mile." I'm deeply grateful to have enjoyed the innovation and discipline of this lifetime "scrapper." His contributions to my life then and now are invaluable.

Dewayne Thompson — This man is more than a teacher, he's an "Experience." While many students during my college days avoided taking his business classes because of the rigor and discipline required to succeed, I scooped up every opportunity to be around him. I knew he would pour his whole heart into guiding our learning experience. It has always been a high priority of his to help grow others being intolerant of mediocrity while helping them reach out to achieve their God-given potential. I'm forever grateful for Dr. Dewayne Thompson's friendship and consideration in leaving his door of instruction open for me to continue learning. He is a true mentor and friend.

Reen & Linda Waterman — My heartfelt gratitude to this tremendous couple for their exceptional editing work and assistance. Their diligence, kindness, and insightful contributions have been instrumental in shaping this book. Thank you for your unwavering support and dedication throughout this journey.

ABOUT THE AUTHOR

With over 30 years of marketplace experience, Chad Carter has built a distinguished career as a business leader in human resources and communications. His expertise spans leading roles at top-tier organizations, including the U.S. Pet Care Division of Mars, Sony Music, and a consulting practice serving healthcare providers in Nashville, TN. Known for his practical approach, he excels at identifying real business challenges and driving actionable solutions.

His deep industry knowledge is further reflected in his service as a Chairman and Executive Coach for C12 Business Forums. He also contributes as a Consultant in Executive Search for Mission:Leadership and to shaping the next generation of business leaders through his role on the Lee University Advisory Board for the School of Business.

A recognized authority on hiring, Chad is the author of *Essentials of Hiring: The Five Attributes* and creator of **The Predictive Hiring Model**, a groundbreaking framework designed to transform hiring processes and drive exceptional results. He shares these strategies through workshops and consulting, equipping organizations with the tools to make profoundly better hiring decisions.

www.PredictiveHiringModel.com

ALSO BY CHAD CARTER

In *The Five Attributes: Essentials of Hiring*, Chad Carter offers insight and instruction from his 30+ years in human resources and consulting. He casts a bright light on five essential attributes for "WHAT" every hiring manager must intentionally study in each interviewee with a "no compromise" approach.

Considering that two-thirds of all hiring decisions are hiring mistakes, Carter connects with the need that a radical change is necessary. The Five Attributes is the first in a series of tools that provide solutions to overcome the current problems inherent in hiring. Ultimately, Carter inspires greater confidence in the hiring manager to achieve predictive hiring success.

AVAILABLE FROM
www.PredictiveHiringModel.com

PREDICTIVE HIRING TOOLKIT

Have all the resources you need to implement The Predictive Hiring Model within your organization.

Toolkit includes:

Predictive Hiring Assessment Tool

Candidate Hiring Scorecard

The Ideal Candidate Profile

Interviewing and Hiring eBook

Predictive Hiring Model with all 6 Disciplines

Introductory Interview Questions

Interview Protocol — Director Level and Above

Interview Agenda Example

Offer Letter Example

Organizational Announcement Example

Many Other Resources

TOOLKIT AVAILABLE AT
www.PredictiveHiringModel.com

CONNECT WITH CHAD

To learn more about Chad's **speaking**, **consulting**, and **coaching**,
visit www.PredictiveHiringModel.com
or contact him via:

Email: chadcartertn@gmail.com

Linkedin: linkedin.com/in/chadcarter

X: @chadcarter.com

Instagram: @chadcartertn

Phone: 615-585-0552

Looking forward to hearing from you!